THE

ESSENTIAL

JAZZ

RECORDINGS

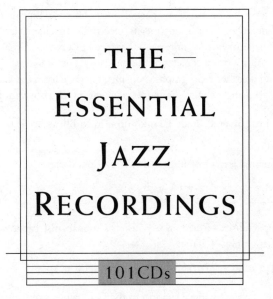

— THE —
ESSENTIAL
JAZZ
RECORDINGS

101CDs

ROSS PORTER

McCLELLAND & STEWART

Library and Archives Canada Cataloguing in Publication

Porter, Ross
    The essential jazz recordings : 101 CDs / Ross Porter.

ISBN-13: 978-0-7710-7032-7
ISBN-10: 0-7710-7032-2

    1. Compact discs – Reviews. 2. Music – Compact disc catalogs.
3. Jazz – Discography. I. Title.

ML156.9.P847 2006   016.78165'0266   C2006-901908-8

We acknowledge the financial support of the Government of Canada through the Book Publishing Industry Development Program and that of the Government of Ontario through the Ontario Media Development Corporation's Ontario Book Initiative. We further acknowledge the support of the Canada Council for the Arts and the Ontario Arts Council for our publishing program.

Typeset in Janson by M&S, Toronto
Printed and bound in Canada

McClelland & Stewart Ltd.
75 Sherbourne Street
Toronto, Ontario
M5A 2P9
www.mcclelland.com

2   3   4   5   10 09 08 07

This book is lovingly dedicated to my role model,
my father, T.C. Porter,
and to my late mother, Doreen Porter,
whose love of music pointed the way.

Contents

Preface

Many of us can remember when we first discovered music, whether a particular artist or a group or orchestra, and some of us have been lucky enough to discover a whole genre and know from the first moments that this was the sound that most moved us. I can't remember the exact moment, but I first discovered jazz as a child. I was one of those kids who used to lie awake at night listening to a transistor radio hidden under my pillow. In the days before Walkmans or iPods, when sound wasn't confined to an ear piece, this is how you muffled the noise and tried to fool your parents into thinking you were asleep. Radio was the primary medium for music for those of us too young or too far away to buy records or to listen to live performances, and transistor radios were the first step in the long march toward making recorded music not just mobile but private. I spent hours listening to that transistor, creeping along the dial from station to station until some snatch of a song arrested me. I stopped for sounds that I responded to emotionally, that aroused in me a feeling of awe that I still experience today when I hear good music. I learned only later that it was jazz that did this to me. All I knew was that I was hooked.

As a teenager I worked at the Treble Clef, a record store in Ottawa, where I found the old CTI (Creed Taylor International) catalogue, which introduced jazz to me in a whole new way. More mature then, and with a deeper appreciation of how music is made, I learned to listen properly to the songs and tunes that accompanied my life, and the ability to really hear the nuances has served me ever since, no matter what music I am listening to. Jazz can do that. Listening to it carefully, noting the interplay of instruments and of voice or the way a solo takes flight and how it returns to its nest, can lead you to a deeper appreciation of the genre and other genres of music as well.

Jazz is hard to define in a few words because it takes so many forms, and it's this difficulty to categorize it easily that allows so many to enjoy it, whether listening to a new discovery or an old favourite. To me, jazz is appealing because it represents truth and beauty. To my ears there is nothing more delightful than a swinging blues played by artists in complete accord with one another. There is nothing more exquisite than a solo that explores and extends and bends the melody in a journey to who knows where the first time you hear it. As an art form, jazz has meat on its bones, and it makes for a very rich meal indeed.

One of the most appealing things about jazz is its ability to define who we are, and just as we are constantly redefining ourselves, so too is jazz. It's an art form that spanned the most tumultuous century in history, and looks like it will be with us for as long as there are human beings expressing themselves through music. In fact, jazz music's popularity continues to grow. A number of jazz stations have arisen in the past decade or so; new, exemplary artists continue to arrive on the scene, exploring and innovating in this art form; and jazz continues to enjoy crossover appeal. There are always new listeners who don't quite know where to start. Despite what some would have you believe, jazz is accessible to everyone, and can be enjoyed by everyone. Once you know what it has to offer, you will know whether you get more pleasure from the swinging tunes of big bands or the more unpredictable sounds of free jazz.

In order to appreciate any jazz, you need a sense of fun, adventure, and a desire to take risks. I crave music that grabs my attention. And every album I recommend in this book does just that. When I hear a great album, the easiest way I can describe it is to say that it feels like Christmas. It gives me a feeling of wonder, appreciation, and, there's no other way to put it, it makes me feel good. What's the test of a superior album? Well, to me, if it still sounds terrific years later, and I find I listen to it repeatedly, it's got to be good.

I was asked recently if I could have any job I wanted, what it would be. The answer was easy – I have it. I think I've always had it. I first wrote about jazz for the *Winnipeg Free Press*, then made documentaries on jazz and pop culture for CBC Radio and Television, and for ten years I hosted CBC Radio Two's daily national jazz program, *Afterhours*. Then I was fortunate to be asked to launch CoolTV, Canada's 24/7 jazz channel, and I am currently the president and CEO of what truly is Canada's premier jazz station, JAZZ.FM91 in Toronto. In forty years of working as a broadcaster, being a critic and a fan, I've listened to twenty-five thousand albums in all genres, and I still go back to listen to many of them. So, it has not been easy to whittle my recommendations down to just 101 essential CDs. There are easily 1001 I might have chosen just because I enjoy them, but I tried to keep in mind that I was looking for essential recordings.

What is an essential jazz collection? To me, essential means something basic, something that's a necessity in order to achieve a true understanding of, in this case, jazz as an art form. And to truly understand something, you have to know where it came from and what it is becoming. This is especially true for jazz, which is so rich, varied, and in my opinion, limitless. So, I decided to organize the 101 selections I made after hours and hours of difficult deliberation in more or less chronological order, based on the date the album was first recorded or the first date of a compilation album representing an entire era or career. Even if you don't listen to the CDs in the order I've presented them, I hope that I've been able to convey in words a sense of how jazz has developed.

I've begun with a few albums from the early years of jazz, but there are many more selections from the 1940s, 1950s, and 1960s, known to some as the golden age of jazz. This is when jazz made its sharp turn from dance music, from swing, to listening music, to bebop and hard bop. But during those years, all forms of jazz were alive and kicking, and you will find many of them represented here. Since then, as you'll see, other forms have arisen: fusion, cool, free, and avant-garde, just to name a few, and you'll find selections here that represent most of these forms.

Not everyone is going to agree with my selections. (There are jazz snobs, whose attitude I dislike, who hold one form of jazz superior to another.) But I appreciate most of its forms, and the criteria I've used is not whether this CD is better than that, this form superior to the other, but whether the music is enjoyable, whether it reveals something about the people who made it, about the form and the era in which it was made, and whether people will want to listen to it repeatedly.

It's my hope that you will take a chance on many of these recommendations and that each one leads you to another by that musician or that group or by one of the musicians in the group whose sound has impressed you. Use the book as a guide, but also use it as a springboard. You may find, as I have, that jazz is the perfect accompaniment for your life.

DJANGO REINHARDT, 1910–53
The Best of Django Reinhardt
Recorded in various locations, 1936–48

Jean Baptiste, or Django, Reinhardt was a nomadic, outlandish, self-taught musician who couldn't read music or words. His towering contribution to music makes him one of the most influential jazz guitarists of all time and the single most important jazz musician to emerge from Europe.

Those who worked with him say Reinhardt was ingenious, charming, capricious, and exasperating. He kept a pet monkey, and he was a habitual gambler who once permanently abandoned his new car on the side of the road when it ran out of gas. Many fans will recognize Reinhardt as the source of Sean Penn's musical quest in the Woody Allen movie *Sweet and Lowdown*.

Reinhardt was born in a gypsy caravan in Belgium, and Django is his Roma name. He was a child prodigy on the banjo-guitar, but at age eighteen his playing career almost ended when his left hand and right side from waist to knee were badly burned in a caravan fire. He was bedridden in a nursing home for eighteen months while he recovered. It was while he was there that he developed a new fingering for playing the guitar that primarily used the two fingers of his left hand that had flexibility. His fourth and fifth fingers were permanently curled towards his palm because the tendons had shrunk in the heat of the fire and he could use them only on the first two strings of the guitar. When he soloed, Reinhardt used his index and middle fingers. These limitations shaped his distinctive style as a guitarist.

Reinhardt came into prominence in 1934 with the formation of the Quintette du Hot Club de France. Reinhardt's musical partner in the group was violinist Stéphane Grappelli. Until Grappelli's departure from France and from the quintet at the outbreak of war in 1939, they created some of the most innovative and imaginative music in jazz.

It is estimated that Reinhardt recorded somewhere between 750 to 1,000 sides in his lifetime. A quick survey of releases under his name today shows numerous CDs drawn from a variety of settings, including radio broadcasts, studio sessions, and concerts. For the new fan there is a lot to dive into. A strong place to start is the *The Best of Django Reinhardt*. It features eighteen selections recorded between 1936 and 1948. The music ranges from sensual to high octane.

This is thoroughly charming music that, despite the archival recording sound, deserves to be listened to intently. Reinhardt loved the sound of North American jazz and somehow managed to turn it into something sexy and very European by incorporating gypsy melodies, Russian balalaika music, the French musette, and an abundance of string instruments.

The Hot Club is represented on the CD with four selections, including the uptempo classic "Minor Swing," a song co-written with Grappelli and loosely based on an Eastern European theme ("Dark Eyes"). The raucous "Limehouse Blues" showcases Reinhardt and Grappelli's virtuosity on their respective instruments. "Naguine" is a beautifully relaxed song named after Reinhardt's second wife. The biggest departure for Reinhardt is "Manoir de mes rêves (a.k.a. Django's Castle)," which is the surviving fragment of a symphony he wrote. It features Reinhardt in a session, not long after the end of the Second World War, when he toured the United States, playing with a group of American musicians.

Reinhardt died at the age of forty-three of a cerebral hemorrhage in Samois-sur-Seine, the small town where he had retired. Each year, the town holds a festival to celebrate his music.

Blue Note #37138

ARTIE SHAW, 1910–2004
Highlights From Self Portrait
Recorded in New York and Los Angeles, 1937–1954

Artie Shaw was one of the most colourful and popular jazz musicians in the 1930s and 1940s. Shaw was also opinionated, litigious, and cantankerous, but more importantly he possessed a brilliant mind and was a gifted musician. He was married eight times, and his wives included Betty Kern (the daughter of composer Jerome Kern), novelist Kathleen Winsor, and actresses Lana Turner, Ava Gardner, and Evelyn Keyes. This made him a great subject for the 1985 Academy Award–winning documentary, *Time Is All You've Got*, by Toronto filmmaker Brigitte Berman.

Artie was born Arthur Arshawsky, the son of immigrant parents who worked in the clothing business in New York City. When he was fourteen, he taught himself to play the sax, and a few months later the clarinet. At age fifteen, Shaw left home to play music full time. In the late 1930s, he formed his own band, and was one of the first bandleaders to include a string section in his orchestra.

Shaw's music helped to define the swing era and at the peak of his success he sold more than 100 million records and was earning $60,000 a week. His first hit, "Begin the Beguine," was intended to be a B-side of a recording. But fans loved it so much, it topped the charts for six weeks in 1938. It made Shaw famous at the age of twenty-eight. Unhappy with stardom, Shaw walked away from the music business on numerous occasions, each time reinventing his musical approach. He finally retired from performing in 1954 at age forty-four when he put the clarinet away for good. Shaw said he stepped down for his survival and sanity, because he could no longer play the perfect music he heard in his head.

Self Portrait consists of fourteen tracks pulled from a larger, five-CD box set compiled by Shaw in 2001. The selections were recorded between 1937 and 1954 and include his most famous songs, "Nightmare," "Begin the Beguine," "Stardust," and "Frenesi."

Unlike the other band themes of the time, his 1938 theme song, "Nightmare," is neither bouncy nor upbeat, instead it is dark and brooding, and Shaw's clarinet sounds delightfully ominous.

Shaw achieved much of his success by swinging the American songbook of the era. He took the best standards and gave them a classic form. His interpretation of Gershwin's "Summertime" is open-minded and endlessly fascinating. Shaw's need or desire to surprise people musically was one of his most appealing qualities as a musician.

"Any Old Time" features Billie Holiday on vocals. Shaw hired her as a singer at a time when most white bandleaders refused to hire blacks.

The album's standout track is the striking "Frenesi," a song by Alberto Dominguez that Shaw heard when he disappeared for two months to Mexico in the fall of 1939. His playing is highly musical but the real innovation rests with the string arrangement. Pleasing surprises are the inclusion of "Scuttlebutt" and "Bewitched, Bothered and Bewildered" from 1954 sessions by the Gramercy Five. The big band era was certainly over by then, knocked out of the ring by rock and roll, but Shaw resurfaced that year, for the last time, with a compact bop-sounding group that featured Hank Jones on piano. It was his last recording.

■

Bluebird RCA #63845

BENNY GOODMAN, 1909–86
The Famous 1938 Carnegie Hall Jazz Concert
Recorded in New York City, January 1938

David Goodman, a Jewish immigrant from Hungary who worked in the Chicago stockyards, died in an accident when his son, Benny, was just sixteen. The trauma of losing his hardworking father only hardened Goodman's resolve to make a success of himself, and today he is universally regarded as the epitome of clarinet players.

As a bandleader, Goodman's insistence on perfection – and intolerance for anything less – was legendary. So was his lifelong reluctance to part with a dollar, even after he became a very rich man, especially when negotiating salaries with his musicians. The turnover in the band was high, but the departures were not always about money. Musicians who delivered rarely had trouble with him; it was those who didn't deliver, who didn't try hard enough, who found themselves on the receiving end of the famous "Goodman ray," as it was called. It was an unnerving look that levelled anyone feeling the least guilty or uncertain. One big band reviewer noted that the "ray" was more of "a fish stare," as Benny would not so much look *at* a person as look *through* him.

No one admitted more readily to being preoccupied with perfection than Goodman himself. In George T. Simon's book *The Big Bands*, Goodman is quoted as saying, "I'll never be satisfied with any band. I guess I just expect too much from my musicians, and when they do things wrong, I get brought down." Simon noted that, unlike bandleaders Tommy Dorsey and Glenn Miller, Goodman seldom blew his top at his musicians. "His method was more subtle. When a musician displeased him, Benny would usually just ignore him, a sort of negative method of informing the musician that he was in trouble. Frequently the situation would become so uncomfortable that the musician would quit."

The most regrettable parting-of-the-ways between Benny Goodman and one of his sidemen had its beginnings in one of the greatest swing band triumphs in history – the band's concert at Carnegie Hall in 1938. During the concert, drummer Gene Krupa suddenly broke out of a somewhat slow beat laid down by Benny Goodman and set a new groove for the band that continued without let-up until Krupa began the now-famous tom-tomming that kicked off "Sing, Sing, Sing." Krupa led chorus after chorus, taking the whole band to a blazing climax, with Benny and he playing alone on clarinet and drums.

But it was a bittersweet achievement. Krupa and Goodman had been having disagreements over their approaches to music for some time, and Krupa had been getting his own share of national publicity, which likely didn't sit well with Benny. Mere weeks after the concert, Krupa announced he was leaving the band.

The Carnegie Hall concert was a milestone, as it was the first time jazz was performed in the august venue of a major concert hall. But a craze for swing music had been spreading for a couple of years, giving birth to a new dance, the jitterbug, and the concert was sold out weeks in advance. As the album notes put it, "The tremendous popularity of 'King of Swing' Goodman . . . made him just the man to take 'America's indigenous art form' into the rarefied setting of its concert hall Mecca. And after Goodman strode onto the stage, jazz would be accorded the respect its practitioners and fans knew it warranted."

This exceptional double CD brings it all back – Harry James, Count Basie, Teddy Wilson, Lionel Hampton, Gene Krupa, Cootie Williams, Bobby Hackett, and many others – playing the unparalleled Goodman arrangements of Count Basie's "One O'Clock Jump," with sizzling solos by pianist Jess Stacy and trumpeter Harry James; the Fletcher Henderson gem "Sometimes I'm

Happy," missing from the first issue of the record; Duke Ellington's "Blue Reverie," featuring the remarkable soprano sax technique of Johnny Hodges; Goodman's house specialty "Stompin' at the Savoy"; and the band's super-charged version of Louis Prima's amazing "Sing, Sing, Sing," brought home by Goodman on the clarinet hitting top A followed by a high C.

This expanded, third edition presents the concert in real time and with the finest possible sound quality, thanks to painstaking application of the most modern tools available. The audience's thunderous reaction to rare and dazzling choruses, which were edited out of previous editions, are on this recording, and the glorious resonance of Carnegie Hall is evident throughout. This is an essential swing album to have.

■ ──

Sony BMG Legacy #065143

■

BILLIE HOLIDAY, 1915–59
The Commodore Master Takes
Recorded in New York City, April 1939 and April 1944

A perceptive jazz fan once commented that when Ella Fitzgerald sang about her man leaving, you thought he'd gone to the corner store to pick up a loaf of bread and a carton of milk. When Billie Holiday sang that her man had left, you knew he'd packed a suitcase, caught an airplane, and was never coming back. Therein lies the power of Billie Holiday. She is the most emotionally tragic singer in the history of jazz.

Holiday was born in 1915 in Baltimore. Her real name was Eleanora Fagan Gough. She came up with the name Billie Holiday from the first name of the silent-movie actress Billy Dove and the last name of her father, Clarence Holiday. Her life was one of tragedy. Rape, prostitution, beatings, addiction, incarceration, racism, and divorce were just some of the calamities she experienced. She was the voice of tears and dark memories.

The recordings Holiday made for Commodore Records are some of the most important of her career. All sixteen songs are collected on the *Commodore Master Takes* and represent four recording sessions, one from 1939 and three from 1944.

Commodore began as a small Manhattan electronics store that gradually started selling records. While still running his store, Milt Gabler (comedian Billy Crystal's uncle) moved into the music business by releasing records by Pee Wee Russell, Eddie Condon, and Louis Jordan.

In 1939, Holiday was hired to perform at Café Society, in Greenwich Village, New York's first integrated nightclub outside

Harlem. It was there she premiered "Strange Fruit," which was written by Abel Meeropol, a Jewish high school teacher, that became her signature song. Its lyrics describe a lynched black man hanged from a poplar tree in the American south. The first jazz song to decry racism in the States, its effect on listeners was (and still is) absolutely chilling.

At the time, Holiday was signed to Columbia Records, but both the label's executives and her producer, John Hammond, refused to record the song, perhaps because they didn't want to upset their southern distributors. Holiday contacted her friend Milt Gabler and asked if he would do it. In a daring move, Gabler agreed, and on April 20, 1939, Holiday recorded "Strange Fruit." When you listen to it, you can easily understand why *Time* magazine hailed "Strange Fruit" as the most important song of the twentieth century and why *Q*, a British music magazine, named it one of the ten songs to have actually changed the world.

Holiday went on to record "Strange Fruit" several more times in her career but this is the first and definitive version. She and the band sparkle because they had been playing the song almost every night at Café Society. Pianist Sonny White's playing is dark and rich; Holiday's voice, at age twenty-four, is sombre and pure.

The other selections included on the *Commodore Master Takes* are also impressive. Holiday's slightly autobiographical composition "Fine and Mellow," about a man who drinks, gambles, and womanizes, is powerful and unnerving. Her renditions of "Embraceable You," "I'll Get By," "He's Funny That Way," and "I'll Be Seeing You" are all highly expressive. Much like Louis Armstrong, Holiday makes every song, even familiar classics, hers. There is such power and melancholy in her delivery, you believe each song was written specifically for her. The harsh tone and roughness that affected her voice later in her career is nowhere to be heard. This CD features a vibrant and emotional young singer; it is the essential Billie Holiday disc to own.

Verve/GRP #3145432722

NAT KING COLE, 1919–65
The Best of the Nat King Cole Trio: The Vocal Classics, Vol. 1
Recorded in Los Angeles, 1942–46

I believe that almost everything Nat King Cole recorded is, in varying degrees, worth listening to. He was the consummate professional musician with impeccable vocal delivery, and as a pianist, he was the perfect accompanist to his own singing. Cole personified musical elegance, and his warm voice inhabits all the nooks and crannies of a song.

From 1947 until his death in 1965, he was a hugely successful pop singer who achieved many of the same artistic successes as Frank Sinatra. They both had hit records, shared arrangers and the same record company, and had shows on both television and radio. But unlike Sinatra, who had grown from being a boy singer in big band during the swing era, Cole emerged as a jazz pianist fronting his own group and only then started singing.

Born in 1919 in Montgomery, Alabama, Cole's family moved to Chicago when he was four, and he later sang and played in his father's church – and often snuck out late at night to listen to jazz being performed in the local clubs. His principal influence at the time was the great stride pianist Earl Hines. Cole started performing jazz piano in Chicago in the 1930s and was thought of as a hot contender. At seventeen, he joined a touring musical, but when a cast member absconded with the proceeds in Long Beach, California, Cole found himself stranded there. Playing as many gigs as he could get, Cole soon raised enough money to settle in Southern California.

The idea for the Nat King Cole Trio grew out of cramped stage conditions in a club. There was no room for a drummer to set up, so when Cole was invited to lead his own band at the club, he settled for a piano, bass, and guitar. His reputation as a pianist grew through concerts organized by Norman Granz and recording sessions with two jazz giants, tenor sax player Dexter Gordon and alto sax player Lester Young.

The story of how Cole became a vocalist has a few versions. The most plausible is that he started singing one night at a club because a drunken patron insisted on hearing a vocal version of "Sweet Lorraine." The drunk tipped the trio fifteen cents, five cents for each man. When he asked for a second song, and Cole said he didn't know any others, the drunk reputedly asked for his money back.

As good as Cole was as a pianist and bandleader, he soon realized that his voice provided him with the most potential to become a star. In 1943, he signed with the label that songwriter Johnny Mercer co-founded the previous year, Capitol Records. He stayed with the label until his death in 1965.

The Best of the Nat King Cole Trio: The Vocal Classics showcases twenty-one jazz songs Cole recorded for Capitol from 1942 to 1946. These songs, such as "Frim Fram Sauce," "(Get Your Kicks On) Route 66," "It's Only a Paper Moon," and "Sweet Lorraine" were recorded prior to Cole becoming a pop star, and they qualify as some of the most important of his career.

Cole's first single was inspired by one of his father's sermons. "Straighten Up and Fly Right" was a novelty tune based on a southern folktale about a monkey that hitched a ride on a buzzard and refused to let go. At the time, 1944, money was tight, and Cole sold the rights to song publisher Irving Miller for fifty dollars. The song received extensive airplay and was a huge hit.

The perennial favourite, "It's Only a Paper Moon," begins with beautiful block chords, modulates into a thirty-two-bar vocal

refrain in the middle, and then ends with an instrumental chorus
– just like swing era dance band.

Cole agreed to record "Route 66" in 1946 without ever
hearing it, based solely on songwriter Bobby Troup's reputation
and the tune's hip-sounding title. Cole's timing was perfect; post-
war America loved the song's celebration of travel and of being
free of obligations.

On these songs, Cole's innovative, drummerless trio provided
the only accompaniment, and the improvisational interplay
between Cole on piano, Johnny Miller on bass, and Oscar Moore on
guitar is effortless, as though they were reading one another's minds.
Cole's ability to play great piano lines behind (his own) vocals is the
sound and support every singer wants from their accompanist. As a
vocalist, his careful phrasing and intimate mood is unparalleled.

Cole fans treasure these recordings. As successful as the later
pop hits, such as "Unforgettable," "L-O-V-E," "Those Hazy
Crazy Days of Summer," and "Mona Lisa" were, it was this time
in Cole's career that influenced the influencers. These recordings
have inspired many artists, including Oscar Peterson and Diana
Krall, both of whom used his concept of the trio – piano, bass, and
guitar – as the foundation for their groups.

■ _____

Blue Note #33571

CHARLIE PARKER, 1920–55
Yardbird Suite: The Ultimate Charlie Parker
Recorded in New York and Los Angeles, 1945–52

Charlie "Yardbird" Parker's contribution to the invention of the style of jazz called bebop makes him one of the most important jazz musicians of all time. To many he's also considered the greatest saxophonist in jazz. As a composer, he was responsible for several songs that have become standards, such as "Ornithology," "Scrapple from the Apple," "Ko-ko," and "Anthology."

While he was one of the most innovative and creative musicians, at the same time he was one of the most unstable artists jazz has known. In 1946, after an evening of heavy drug and alcohol use, Parker returned to his Los Angeles hotel room. A lit cigarette started a fire in his mattress, and Parker caused a disturbance when he ran out into the lobby wearing only his socks. This incident led to Parker being committed to Camarillo State Hospital, a California institution for the mentally ill, for six months. In 1954, back in New York, he attempted suicide twice before being admitted to Bellevue Psychiatric Hospital.

Growing up in Kansas City, Parker was so taken by the music scene there that he dropped out of school when he was fourteen to play full time. The following year, he married his first wife and started using heroin. In 1937, he joined Jay McShann's band. Along the way he acquired the nickname Yardbird, later shortened to Bird. The nickname either came from Parker's fondness for chicken (*yardbird* is a southern word for chicken) or from the way he played, flying quickly over the keys on his alto sax.

In 1939, Parker pawned a friend's clarinet to buy a bus ticket to New York City, and in time he became involved in jam sessions at a club in Harlem called Minton's Playhouse. It was there Parker and trumpet player Dizzy Gillespie, among others, took the big band music of the swing era and refashioned it, paring away pop melodies and adding back extended chord-based improvisations as a key feature. This was bebop. It caught on right away among jazz musicians eager for new horizons.

Even to the seasoned jazz fan, the number of CDs in the Charlie Parker catalogue can be overwhelming. A great place to start is with the mind-blowing *The Yardbird Suite: The Ultimate Charlie Parker*, which consists of thirty-eight songs recorded on a double CD.

The set starts in 1945 with one of the greatest musical collaborations in jazz, Parker's recordings with Dizzy Gillespie. The classics "Salt Peanuts," "Hot House," and "Groovin' High" are here. The spontaneous interaction of Parker and Gillespie sounds as if they shared the same heartbeat.

There are other songs jazz fans will recognize. The ironically titled "Relaxin' at the Camarillo" was recorded in Los Angeles after Parker's stay at the institution. Parker's frantic "Moose the Mooche" was named for one of his drug connections; "Yardbird Suite" is a melodic, mid-tempo version of a song Parker wrote as a teenager called "What Price Love"; "Ornithology" was based on "How High the Moon." All three tunes feature a very young Miles Davis on the frontline, playing trumpet.

The genuine longevity of these recordings is a testament to their importance to jazz. Many of them define this innovative era in jazz and show bebop at its pinnacle. They are quite simply some of the best jazz recordings ever made. Miraculously, even strung out on drugs and alcohol, Parker was able to perform at the highest creative level.

Besides the musical brilliance, what makes this package essential to own is that it is the first multi-label "best of" compilation to be released. The "best of" packages that came before it had been put out by one label to promote one artist's essential tracks. For Rhino to prepare this retrospective, six labels participated: Guild, Savoy, Columbia, Musicraft, Dial, and Clef (Verve).

On March 12, 1955, Charlie Parker died while watching jugglers on Tommy Dorsey's TV variety show at New York's Stanhope Hotel in the apartment of his friend and patron, Baroness Pannonica "Nica" de Koenigswarter. The coroner identified his body as being that of a male close to sixty. Parker was thirty-four. He died broke.

In February 2005, in a stroke of irony, Parker's alto sax, which he often pawned when he needed fast cash, was sold for more than a quarter of a million dollars.

■ ─────────────────────────────────────

Rhino #72260

■

LOUIS ARMSTRONG, 1901–71
Louis Armstrong: An American Icon
Recorded in various locations, 1948–68

Louis "Satchmo" Armstrong has been called the most influential musician of the twentieth century. His magnificent career as a trumpet player, singer, and bandleader has made him a legend, and his influence on jazz and popular music is impossible to overstate. He travelled the world, playing for presidents and royalty, yet he and his wife chose to live in a modest house in a working-class neighbourhood in Queens, New York.

Armstrong's talent was a rare combination of instrumental, comedic, compositional, and vocal ability. Add to that a healthy dose of charisma and charm that helped put his act across to all audiences, white and black, young and old. When Louis performed, he wore a smile a mile wide. He repeatedly punctuated his singing by mopping the sweat from his brow with a pocket handkerchief, and he delighted fans with his sandpapery singing voice and his merry mangling of the English language.

Born in New Orleans, Armstrong learned to play the cornet at reform school. He played in several New Orleans bands before joining Joe "King" Oliver's Creole Jazz Band in Chicago in 1922. By making this move to Chicago, and shortly thereafter to New York, Armstrong took a regional dance music, fronted by brass instruments, and introduced it to the world. And the world, then recovering from the First World War and accustomed to dancing to orchestras and a languid 2/4 rhythm, fell in love with Armstrong's jazz and its 4/4 beat. Along with the jaunty rhythms of ragtime jazz, Armstrong also brought north scat singing – the singing of wordless phrases or nonsense words – and introduced the jazz solo, all of which revolutionized popular music.

For most of his life, Armstrong toured relentlessly, sometimes doing 300 performances a year. His recordings span almost fifty years, and comprise more than a thousand songs. In the 1960s and 1970s, his was one of the most recognizable faces in the world. When he died in his sleep on July 6, 1971, at the age of seventy, approximately 25,000 people waited in line to pay their respects.

For those discovering Armstrong for the first time, the best place to start is *Louis Armstrong: An American Icon*. This three-CD set features selections from the last three decades of Armstrong's life and includes songs recorded for Decca, ABC-Paramount, RCA, Verve, Columbia, Roulette, Mercury, and Kapp. Disc one features the small group music Armstrong recorded from 1946 to 1954, such as "Do You Know What It Means to Miss New Orleans," "That Lucky Old Sun," and "A Kiss to Build a Dream On." The second disc includes songs from 1954 to 1956, including duets with Ella Fitzgerald and the hits "Mack the Knife," "When You're Smiling," "Blueberry Hill," and "Lazy River." The third and final disc covers 1956 to 1968. This is the Louis those of us of a certain age remember and includes the hits "Hello Dolly" and "What a Wonderful World."

■ ───

Universal/HIP-O #40138

LOUIS ARMSTRONG, 1901–71
Louis Armstrong Plays W.C. Handy
Recorded in Chicago, July 1954

When Louis Armstrong played the trumpet, he pointed the bell toward the heavens, and the stage lights danced on the horn's polished finish. To some, Armstrong was a great musician, to others he was the consummate entertainer.

The road Armstrong took to becoming one of the most popular entertainers in the world was extremely bumpy. When he was born on August 4, 1901, there was no indication he was headed for greatness; his future looked bleak. His father, William, abandoned the family during Armstrong's infancy, and he spent the first years of his life living with his grandmother. After age five, he lived with his mother in stark poverty on the fringe of the New Orleans red-light district. It would have been easy for him to have become hardened and cynical, just another poor boy gone wrong. But instead he discovered music.

In the early days of Armstrong's career he was known as a trumpet player who sang. But as the years wore on, his lips and health wore down. The public now knew him better as a singer who played the trumpet. His talent and abilities as an entertainer, however, didn't diminish.

As great as he was, Armstrong did have his detractors. Many beboppers, who came to dominate jazz in the 1950s and 1960s, looked down on his music and stage antics. They considered his music to be conservative, traditional, and played by mouldy figs. For them, the performance and integrity of their music was all that mattered. For Satchmo, bebop was just another variation on a theme, and he was determined to hold his musical course.

In 1954, Armstrong's recording contract with Decca ended. George Avakian, a producer at Columbia, approached Joe Glaser, Louis's manager, with the idea of recording an album of the songs of W.C. Handy. Handy was the blind father of the blues and wrote many songs that have become blues standards, such as "St. Louis Blues," "Beale St. Blues," and "Memphis Blues." Glaser agreed to the session, but Avakian would have to record in Chicago during a three-day break in Satchmo's touring schedule.

It was a remarkable concept, the music of W.C. Handy, the founder of the blues, and Louis Armstrong, the greatest musician ever to play a trumpet. Eleven songs were recorded with the Armstrong's All Stars: Trummy Young on trombone, Arvell Shaw on bass, Barney Bigard on clarinet, Billy Kyle on piano, Barrett Deems on drums, and Velma Middleton on vocals.

Armstrong's straightforward vocals put across the story in the songs, and his trumpet playing matches their emotional depths. He was still taking the art of the solo to new highs, and the band worked to support the star. The highlight of the album is "St. Louis Blues." Armstrong's version is one of the best ever recorded.

Avakian played the finished tapes from the session for W.C. Handy. In perhaps the best compliment of all, tears of joy streamed from the blues master's sightless eyes. He never thought he would hear his blues played as well as this.

■ ──

Sony BMG/Legacy #064925

□

BUD POWELL, 1924–66
The Best of Bud Powell: The Blue Note Years
Recorded in New York and Hackensack, New Jersey, 1949–63

Earl "Bud" Powell's life was unhappy and painful, but his piano playing was exceptional, innovative, and very influential. The grandson of a flamenco guitarist and son of a stride pianist, Powell grew up in New York City. Before turning to jazz at age fifteen, when he joined a band led by his brother, a trumpeter, Powell played classical piano. As a teenager, Powell was a regular at the crucible of bebop, Minton's Playhouse in New York City. It was there he fell under the spell of the bebop innovators Charlie Parker, Thelonious Monk, and Dizzy Gillespie. Before he turned eighteen, Powell had played with Parker and was being mentored by Monk, who became Powell's lifelong friend. In 1944, he made his first record, with a band led by trumpeter Cootie Williams. The album included the premiere recording of Monk's "'Round Midnight."

The following year, at the age of twenty-one, in a racially motivated altercation with the police, Powell was beaten over the head. His personality changed, he started suffering from headaches, and for the rest of his life, he suffered periodic mental breakdowns. Later that year, Powell was institutionalized for the first time. In 1951, he was arrested for possession of narcotics. He was hospitalized for seventeen months and received electroshock treatments. There was another hospital stay in 1959. To escape many of the pressures he was experiencing, and to make a better living as a musician, he moved to Paris in 1959 and stayed until 1964. There he fell ill with tuberculosis. (The character played by Dexter Gordon in the movie *'Round Midnight* was loosely based on Bud Powell.)

To appreciate Bud Powell's greatness, you need to know that in the late 1940s, a great number of pianists played stride, a style that is similar to ragtime but has more syncopation. Powell pioneered a more fluid approach, employing frequent arpeggios (a chord played one note at a time) and unusual, surprising accents. His playing had a huge influence on a younger generation of pianists, including Chick Corea, Keith Jarrett, Bill Evans, and McCoy Tyner.

Unfortunately, Powell's recording career was inconsistent. His mental problems and alcoholism often prevented him from providing his best efforts. But many of the good moments can be found on *The Best of Bud Powell: The Blue Note Years*.

The CD comprises fifteen pieces from 1949–63. "Bouncing with Bud" and "52nd Street Theme" are two of the most influential songs of Powell's career. An all-star quintet, featuring Fats Navarro on trumpet, Sonny Rollins (only eighteen at the time) on tenor sax, Roy Haynes on drums, and Tommy Potter on bass, delivers plenty of fresh ideas in the bop tradition. The gorgeous "Parisian Thoroughfare" is one of Powell's best-loved songs and predates his move to Paris by eight years. Powell's playing is eloquent and powerful. Another well-known number is the athletic bopper "Un Poco Loco," which features Powell in a trio with "Curly" Russell on bass and Max Roach on drums. "Collard Greens and Black-Eyed Peas" is perhaps the most memorable song in the collection. Here, bassist George Duvivier lays down a strong, steady foundation, and Powell's shapely piano playing is one of the highlights of the compilation.

Bud Powell died on August 1, 1966, from a lethal combination of tuberculosis, alcoholism, and malnutrition.

■ ———————————————————————————————

Blue Note #93204

George Shearing, b. 1919

Lullabies of Birdland: A Musical Autobiography

Recorded in New York, Los Angeles, and San Francisco, 1949–2000

Pianist George Shearing is a rarity: a British jazz musician who became a household name in North America after he immigrated to the States in 1947. His distinctive sound featured his unique "locked hands" style of playing the piano, with the guitar and vibraphone playing in close harmony. The sound was immediately appealing to fans and made him a jazz star. His success is all the more remarkable because Shearing was born blind.

His material has been recorded by many artists, including Sarah Vaughan, Duke Ellington, Ella Fitzgerald, Dexter Gordon, Lionel Hampton, Stan Kenton, Charlie Parker, Woody Herman, Bud Powell, Lester Young, Mel Torme, Count Basie, Stan Getz, Erroll Garner, and Miles Davis.

His long career, spanning almost six decades and numerous labels, makes it difficult to recommend just one release. But the double CD *Lullabies of Birdland: A Musical Autobiography* really is an essential set to own. It is made up of twenty-five songs recorded between 1949 and 2000 for numerous labels and released to coincide with the publication of his 2004 autobiography, *Lullaby of Birdland*. Unfortunately what's missing from this compilation is a sampling of the music Shearing recorded for Capitol in the 1950s and early 1960s.

The set starts with "September in the Rain," the song that introduced the distinctive Shearing sound to a large audience in 1949. Its appealing melody hides the important techniques that Shearing was using: his use of distinctive chord voicings in conjunction with guitar and vibraphone; his way of laying back on the beat; and his multi-note phrasing, which bebop players before him had had trouble selling to the public.

In 1952, Shearing was approached by the owners of Birdland, a prominent jazz club in New York, to write a theme song for a nightly six-hour disc-jockey show that they were sponsoring. Shearing went home and, he later said, while eating a steak "The tune came into my head." He finished writing what became his signature song, "Lullaby of Birdland," in ten minutes. Shearing has joked that he continued to buy meat from the same butcher for years.

There are three versions of the song. The first is the 1952 original by the Shearing Quintet. Fast-forward to 1985 for a version featuring Latin percussionist Tito Puente and then on to a sparse live version, with Shearing on piano and Toronto bassist Neil Swainson, that was recorded in Tokyo in 1987.

In 1961, Shearing teamed up with the brothers Wes, Buddy, and Monk Montgomery to record "Darn That Dream." The ensemble, particularly Wes Montgomery's guitar, broadens the scope of the Shearing sound.

One of George's oldest musical friendships was with singer Joe Williams. They first met in the 1940s in Chicago and performed together periodically. Their delightful version of "Heart and Soul" first appeared on Shearing's short-lived 1970s label, Sheba.

By the end of the 1970s, Shearing had signed with Carl Jefferson's California-based label, Concord Records. It was a highly creative and prolific time for Shearing, and more than two-thirds of the material on this compilation comes from that period. Some recordings are sessions done with other Concord artists including singers Mel Torme, Ernestine Anderson, and Carmen McRae. It is the work with Torme that is most satisfying, particularly their comical "New York, New York" medley. Shearing's musically spontaneous sense of humour makes this a very clever piece.

Shearing also made several recordings as half of a duo, including with guitarist Jim Hall, bassist Brian Torff, and pianist Marian McPartland. Shearing and his partners are all highly articulate and, as you might expect, exude sophistication. The set closes with "Fly Me to the Moon," a live recording with Shearing's present-day quintet, recorded at the new Birdland in 2000.

Concord #2211

NORMAN GRANZ, 1918–2001
The Complete Norman Granz Jam Sessions
Recorded in Hollywood and New York, 1952–54

Norman Granz was arguably the most important non-musician in jazz. As the founder of four important labels, Norgan (1946), Clef (1953), Verve (1956), and later Pablo (1973), he created the largest catalogue of jazz ever produced. He attracted many of the major names, including Louis Armstrong, Duke Ellington, Ella Fitzgerald, and Oscar Peterson, to his labels. Granz was fearless in his beliefs and as a promoter, and he cancelled gigs because of racism. In Kansas City, he promoted the first mixed-race dance in the city's history, and in Charleston, South Carolina, he presented the first mixed-race concert. He once pulled his band out of a sold-out concert in New Orleans when he found that the seating was segregated. He encountered strong resistance on one occasion when an upset policeman held a loaded gun to his stomach because he was insisting that white cabdrivers take his artists as customers.

Granz's foray into jazz started in the early 1940s at a Los Angeles club, where he promoted a weekly jam session on Sunday evenings. The premise was simple. Put a group of creative musicians together, turn them loose on blues and standards, and wait for the magic. The jam session was an idea as old as jazz itself, but Ganz's formula consistently created favourable results.

The jam sessions took off and created the template for Granz's future. On July 2, 1944, he sold out a concert at a stuffy classical music venue that was home to the Los Angeles Philharmonic. The recording of that event sold an unexpected 150,000 copies and laid the groundwork for a record company and a concept Granz would use repeatedly. In 1946, he and his noisy cohorts were banned from the hall, but the Jazz at the Philharmonic name stuck. Granz had created one of the most successful touring jazz shows of the time.

The Complete Norman Granz Jam Sessions is a logical extension of the live concerts concept. In 2004, all nine jam session albums were put on five CDs, along with the original cover art, in-depth liner notes, and a sturdy metal slipcase.

Granz creatively blended swing and bebop players on eighteen originals and standards. He never sold musical perfection, so all recordings are first takes, allowing listeners the rare chance to listen to spontaneous improvisation by many of the most gifted musicians in jazz. Several of the originals are uptempo barnburners set to showcase the artists' musical chops. Particularly poignant are the three long ballad medleys.

The sessions took place from 1952 to 1954 in New York City and Hollywood while JATP was touring. The musicians are heard in gatherings of eight or nine players and include pianists Count Basie and Oscar Peterson; Freddie Greene, Herb Ellis, and Barney Kessell on guitar; tenor saxophonists Flip Phillips, Ben Webster, and Stan Getz; Charlie Parker, Johnny Hodges, Benny Carter, and Illinois Jacquet on alto saxophones; Ray Brown on bass; Harry Sweets Edison, Roy Eldrige, Dizzy Gillespie, and Charlie Shavers on trumpet; Buddy DeFranco on clarinet; Buddy Rich and Louis Bellson on drums; and Lionel Hampton on vibes. It is a proud embarrassment of musical riches.

The risk with jam sessions is that they turn into cutting contests, where musicians try to outdo one another. They do that here, but in a way that encouraged each of them to blossom, nudge, inspire, and caress one another musically to achieve the same result. Everyone has a chance to shine. Soloists speak in their own voice, and it would appear no egos were damaged.

This is a grand opportunity to hear jazz history in the making. The cost of a five-CD box set is high, but I guarantee you will return to this release time and time again.

■ _____

Verve #B000325202

HORACE SILVER, b. 1928
Retrospective
Recorded in Hackensack and Englewood Cliffs,
New Jersey; New York; and Los Angeles, 1952–78

Horace Ward Martin Tavares Silver was exposed to lots of different music from a very early age. His Portuguese father and American mother listened to Portuguese and Cape Verdean folk music, and at church he heard the gospel music his mother sang. Later, he listened to blues records from the 1930s and 1940s at home, and in the clubs he heard Latin music. In time, these influences found their way into many of his compositions.

There are two important moments in Silver's evolution as a musician. The first was as a teenager, when an older player gave him the "fake book," a collection of sheet music of popular songs with the chord changes at the top of the page that musicians rely on when playing live. The book gave Silver a much stronger understanding of how to play music. The second was when he heard *Groovin' High* by Charlie Parker and Dizzy Gillespie. It was the first bebop record Silver heard, and it helped him understand the level of playing that would be required to make it as a musician.

Silver was hugely influenced by the music of Bird, Dizzy, and others, but he remained concerned that they were taking the music down the path of musical snobbery to a place that few could understand. In his own compositions, Silver kept the bop feel but added melodies loaded with funk, gospel, and blues.

Silver's music was an important force in jazz around the world. Of the many artists signed to the Blue Note label, he was one of the most valuable, and it was his successful sales that helped to solidify Blue Note as a commercial enterprise. Silver was an extremely prolific composer and one of a few jazz musicians to record albums of almost entirely original material. Many of those songs have become jazz standards.

Horace Silver Retrospective is a four-CD, forty-five-song box set that covers his time with Blue Note from 1952 to 1978. Disc one begins with Silver's first release for the label, with his trio featuring Art Blakey on drums. Of particular note is "Opus De Funk," a great blues tune that mixes elements of bebop, swing, and gospel. The disc also documents the work he did as a member of the Jazz Messengers between 1953 and 1955. Silver's slinky blues, "Doodlin'" and "The Preacher," with a gospel backbeat, are classics. Both the instrumental and vocal versions of the Latin-feeling "Señor Blues" are also included.

The second disc contains three songs from Silver's 1959 classic album *Blowin' the Blues Away*: the title song, the finger poppin' "Sister Sadie," and one of Silver's prettiest melodies, "Peace." From 1960 is the Latin-tinged "Nica's Dream," a tribute to the jazz patron Baroness Pannonica "Nica" de Koenigswarter. "Filthy McNasty" is a funky blues with a great beat that Silver wrote after seeing the 1940 W.C. Fields film, *The Bank Dick*, with the character of that name. Featured prominently on many of the recordings on this disc is trumpet player Blue Mitchell, who brought a great, soulful element to the Silver sound.

The first song on disc three picks up on Silver's father's suggestion that he incorporate some of the Portuguese music he heard as a child. "Song for My Father" is Silver's response. It features a beautiful tenor solo by sax player Joe Henderson. "The Cape Verdean Blues" was based on Portuguese folk music. The energetic, hard bop blues "Psychedelic Sally" features a blistering tenor sax solo by Stanley Turrentine.

I should warn you that there are low points on discs three and four. The least impressive tracks are vocal sessions from the 1970s, when Silver started writing lyrics and using vocalists. As stylish a singer as Andy Bey is, nothing can dig him out of the song about organic food called "Old Mother Nature Calls."

To date *Retrospective* is the only extensive compilation to include all of Silver's celebrated songs. In his salad days, Horace Silver was one of the great jazz composers and created a body of work that is now part of the standard jazz repertoire. *Retrospective* is a fitting testament. Just ignore its drawbacks, as most of the songs included are essential to have.

■

Blue Note #95576

THE MODERN JAZZ QUARTET
Django
Recorded in New York and Hackensack, New Jersey, 1953–55

The Modern Jazz Quartet is one of the most acclaimed and successful small bands in the history of jazz. In order to bring more dignity and sophistication to jazz, the MJQ took a page from classical string quartets. They dressed in tuxedos, rehearsed frequently, and played original elegant and melodic jazz in concert halls, rather than in clubs. Being professional was so important to them, they would even rehearse how they walked on stage.

The MJQ grew out of the Dizzy Gillespie big band of the late forties. From 1946 to 1950, they served as his rhythm section and would play as a quartet to give the other musicians a break from the bandstand. They eventually left Dizzy's band, and by 1952 the Quartet consisted of Milt Jackson on vibes, John Lewis on piano, Percy Heath on bass, and Kenny Clarke (1952–55) on drums.

On and off, the MJQ lasted forty-three years. They recorded frequently for several labels, including Prestige, Atlantic, Verve, and United Artists. The MJQ have the distinction of being the only jazz band ever signed to Apple, the short-lived label the Beatles started in 1968.

In their glory days, the Modern Jazz Quartet functioned as a corporation, with all four members drawing equal salaries and each having an area of responsibility. Lewis was the musical director and wrote most of the music, Jackson took care of promotion, Heath handled the finances, and Connie Kay (who succeeded Kenny Clarke in 1955) was the tour manager.

Their musical awakening can be found on the eight selections that comprise *Django*. The title song is the closest the MJQ ever came to having a hit. Lewis wrote it as a tribute to the French gypsy guitarist Django Reinhardt when he died in 1953. It is a stately piece featuring a playful exchange between piano and vibes.

"One Bass Hit" is a jazz standard written by the MJQ's former employer, Dizzy Gillespie. It is a showcase for bassist Percy Heath, a poetic improviser who says more with fewer notes than most artists. The counterpoint of "The Queen's Fancy" takes you back to the nineteenth century. Lewis is unhurried on piano and brings a melodic grace to the number.

The two principal soloists on *Django* are John Lewis on piano and Milt Jackson on vibes. Lewis was an exceedingly polished musician and one of the most accomplished jazz pianists of his generation. He was fascinated by certain aspects of classical music, and many of his compositions are a marvellous confluence of the two genres. For many, Jackson's vibes was the defining sound of the MJQ. He had a graceful and assured way with such standards as Vernon Duke's "Autumn in New York," but he could also swing with poetic power on George and Ira Gershwin's "But Not For Me." Both musicians make you feel they are imparting valuable information when they play, and that you absolutely need to listen.

■

Concord Prestige #7057-6

FRANK SINATRA, 1915–98
Classic Sinatra: His Great Performances
Recorded in Hollywood, 1953–60

Depending on when you were born, you knew him as Ol' Blue Eyes, the Voice, the Chairman of the Board, or the old guy who sang with Bono. Francis Albert Sinatra set the standard for quality, style, charity, and swagger by which all pop-culture personalities will long be measured. He was also one of the most troubled icons of popular music. He transcended the genre, but he was primarily a jazz singer.

Sinatra was born on December 12, 1915, in Hoboken, New Jersey. It was a difficult birth, and in his effort to deliver the baby by forceps, the doctor ripped Sinatra's left ear, cheek, and neck, and punctured his ear drum. Once delivered, the baby failed to breathe, and the doctor set his body aside to attend to the mother. Only Sinatra's grandmother's quick thinking saved him. She held the baby under cold running water until he cried. It was his first great vocal performance.

Sinatra could swing like no one else. He attracted and worked with the absolute best from the world of jazz: the best arrangers: Quincy Jones, Billy May, Johnny Mandel, Nelson Riddle, Claus Ogerman, Robert Farnon, Neal Hefti, and Gordon Jenkins; the best musicians: Red Norvo, Eddie "Lockjaw" Davis, Harry "Sweets" Edison, Count Basie, Milt Bernhardt, and Duke Ellington; the best songwriters: Antonio Carlos Jobim, Cole Porter, Johnny Mercer, Sammy Cahn, and Jimmy Van Heusen. He influenced the best musicians: Oscar Peterson, Diana Krall, Lester

Young, and Joe Lovano. And he learned from the best: Harry James, Tommy Dorsey, Billie Holiday, and Louis Armstrong.

Never formally trained as a singer, Sinatra grew up amid the blossoming jazz culture, absorbing its attitudes and using its songs. His style grew out of the swing bands of the 1930s and 1940s, and he tried to emulate the most popular singer of the era, Bing Crosby. He got his first break when Harry James hired him for his orchestra, but he left six months later to work in Tommy Dorsey's orchestra. Dorsey's tone on the trombone was pure, his phrasing elegant, with smooth, long legato phrases, and Sinatra learned how to adapt it vocally. After a year and a half of singing with Dorsey, Sinatra discovered the key to his playing. Dorsey was able to breathe in a way that couldn't be seen, out of the side of his mouth. Sinatra was a quick study and his breathing technique, coupled with a quieter, bel canto approach than Crosby's, gave him his distinctive sound.

Between 1954 and 1961, Sinatra recorded thirteen albums for Capitol Records. They represent the zenith of his career. *Classic Sinatra* highlights twenty of those great performances, including "I've Got the World on a String," "Young at Heart," "You Make Me Feel So Young," and "Night and Day."

Sinatra was a songwriter's dream. He had perfect pitch and breath control and understood the importance of nuance. His top notes were soft, his lower notes gentle, and his voice glided with ease through the lyrics, articulating every syllable. Once a song became linked with Sinatra, it crossed over into the pantheon of American popular song, and other singers recorded their versions.

Johnny Mercer's "One for My Baby," the definitive saloon song, became Sinatra's signature. "In the Wee Small Hours of the Morning" is one of the saddest love songs ever written. Bob Hilliard and David Mann had Nat King Cole in mind when they wrote it. The song ended up with Sinatra and features him at his most melancholy and brilliant. Gershwin's "Someone to Watch Over Me" is an extraordinary performance. "I've Got You Under My Skin" is the single greatest recording of his career. Sinatra, a perpetual perfectionist, was not happy until the twenty-second take.

Eighteen of the twenty songs on *Classic Sinatra* were arranged by Nelson Riddle. It is this relationship that ranks as the single most important of Sinatra's musical career. Riddle, a former big band trombonist, understood the singer and gave him space and freedom. He crafted arrangements that suited Sinatra perfectly, and he understood the importance of adding jazz for colour, whether it was a muted trumpet solo by Harry "Sweets" Edison or a blistering trombone solo by Milt Bernhardt. Riddle's, as well as Sinatra's, musical vocabulary came from jazz.

Classic Sinatra is the essential collection of Sinatra's songs.

EMI #23502

■

BEN WEBSTER, 1909–73
Music for Loving: Ben Webster with Strings
Recorded in New York, May 28, 1954, and Amsterdam, the
Netherlands, September 9, 1955

Ben Webster's albums are still among the best in jazz. He was one
of jazz's greatest ballad players, and his well-worn sound on the
tenor saxophone only added a sense of melancholy and sorrow to
the music he played.

Webster learned the violin as a child and in his teens started
performing on the piano, accompanying silent movies. As he
embarked on a career as a professional musician, Webster shifted
to the tenor sax because he felt it best expressed what he had to say
musically. He played with Bennie Moten, Cab Calloway, Fletcher
Henderson, and briefly in the 1930s with Duke Ellington. He
eventually rejoined Ellington's band in 1940 and sat in the saxophone section with one of Ellington's great soloists, the alto sax
player Johnny Hodges. Hodges's technique and musical elegance
had an impact on Webster and helped him develop into one of the
star players in the orchestra. "Cotton Tail" and "All Too Soon"
were two of the songs that showcased his playing. As an added
feature in concert, Ellington sometimes asked him to play the
piano. One night, Webster stayed a little too long at the ivories and
Ellington expressed displeasure at his grandstanding. Afterward, in
protest, Webster cut one of Ellington's suits to bits. Webster left
the orchestra in 1943.

Ben Webster usually wore a fedora that sat rakishly on the
back of his head and was his signature. He was a big drinker of

medium height with a big chest and wide shoulders. He developed a hard exterior, but those who knew him well say he was an emotionally sensitive man who was often moved to tears, weeping at the mere mention of a deceased friend's name. Many were fearful of his temper, particularly when he was woken from a deep sleep. Those who toured with him learned to stand back when they woke him up, as he was prone to using his fists.

His refusal to change his sound to suit the times, as well as years of hotel living, touring, and racial prejudice, collectively took their toll on Webster, and in 1964, he moved permanently to Europe. He was based in Copenhagen and played only when it suited him. On his deathbed in Amsterdam in 1973, Webster left instructions that Ol' Betsy, the tenor saxophone he bought in 1938, was never to be played again. Today it is displayed at the Institute of Jazz Studies at Rutgers University in Newark, New Jersey.

Of the fifty-odd recordings he made, *Music for Loving: Ben Webster with Strings* is one of the most alluring and engaging. It is a double CD, featuring two albums by Webster, *Music with Feeling* and *Music for Loving*. (As a bonus, an album by Harry Carney, Ellington's baritone sax player, *Harry Carney with Strings* has also been included.) The arrangements and conducting were by Billy Strayhorn and Ralph Burns. The players included Strayhorn, Teddy Wilson, and Hank Jones on piano, George Duvivier and Ray Brown on bass, and Louis Bellson and Jo Jones on drums.

It is hard not to feel a surge of inspiration when listening to *Music for Loving*. Webster was a great improviser, and his breathy, sensual tones make this a very sexy CD. "Willow Weep for Me," "Blue Moon," and "Teach Me Tonight" are just a few of the pretty ballads Webster caresses. Like many of the great instrumentalists in jazz, Webster brought a vocal quality to his playing and often memorized the lyrics to the songs he played. On some selections, the place he chose to breathe was the same place singers would choose. Webster's heartbreaking rendition of "Chelsea Bridge," a

powerful ballad he played with Ellington, still sounds fresh.
Despite the passage of time, *Music for Loving* remains a source of
inspiring music.

■───

Verve #3145277742

SARAH VAUGHAN, 1924–90
Sarah Vaughan
Recorded in New York City, December 1954

Sarah Vaughan was a great jazz vocalist, as talented as Ella Fitzgerald or Billie Holiday. What made Vaughan stand out was the broad range of colour in her voice. With a four-octave range, she could reach inside a song and make it her very own.

Vaughan was a singer's singer. She understood jazz because she was a product of the bebop era, learning her craft in the bebop breeding group formed by Earl Hines with singer Billy Eckstine. There she performed alongside Dizzy Gillespie and Charlie Parker. Her style was cheekier than most and earned her the nickname Sassy.

Vaughan had frequent crossover successes with pop tunes such as "Misty," "Broken-Hearted Melody," and "Tenderly." Even when she sang pop, Vaughan still sounded like a jazz singer. She was an original.

Vaughan made many records in her career, but her most satisfying one is her self-titled 1954 album, *Sarah Vaughan*. Ernie Wilkins wrote the brilliant arrangements and they are played by a sparkling band that included Herbie Mann on flute, Paul Quinchette on tenor sax, Jimmy Jones on piano, Joe Benjamin on bass, and Roy Haynes on drums. By far though, it is the twenty-four-year-old virtuoso Clifford Brown on trumpet who stands out, showing off his dexterity but never upstaging Vaughan. Brown would die in a car accident eighteen months later.

The song selection is perfect. Vaughan's smoky voice bops fresh life into the much recorded George Shearing classic "Lullaby of

Birdland." Vernon Duke's "April in Paris" is given a slow, pensive treatment. "I'm Glad There Is You" is Jimmy Dorsey's one and only hit as a songwriter, and Vaughan's performance of this ballad is flawless. Her moving rendition of Kurt Weill's "September Song" is wonderful, and Clifford Brown plays a beautiful solo.

Sarah Vaughan is a perfect record. Vaughan's voice is gorgeous throughout, and she uses a wealth of imaginative vocal phrases and riffs to keep it interesting.

■

Verve #3145433052

COUNT BASIE, 1904–84
April in Paris
Recorded in New York City, July 1955–January 1956

Bill "Count" Basie was one of the great leaders in jazz and played one of its biggest instruments, his orchestra. Basie's big band played so tightly, soloed so imaginatively, and swung so hard it sounded like a small ensemble.

Bill Basie was discovered in Kansas City, but he was born in Red Band, New Jersey, where his mother taught him to play the piano as a child. He was influenced by the early stride piano work of James P. Johnson and Fats Waller. While working as a vaudeville pianist he became stranded in Kansas City and started playing in a movie theatre. In 1928, he joined Walter Page's Blue Devils and later played with the Benny Moten band. Basie formed his own group, the Barons of Rhythm, in 1935, after Moten died, and recruited some of the best players from Moten's band, including Lester Young on sax, vocalist Jimmy Rushing, and trumpet player Oran "Hot Lips" Page.

One night while they were doing a live radio broadcast, jazz producer John Hammond heard them on his car radio in Chicago. It turned out to be a fortuitous audition. Hammond liked what he heard and after seeing Basie live in Kansas City signed him to a recording deal.

It was also on a live broadcast that Basie acquired the nickname Count. One night the host called Basie over to the microphone and said Bill was kind of an ordinary name and now that there was an Earl (Hines) and a Duke (Ellington), wasn't it time to elevate him to Count? The nickname stuck.

The blues and swing were the foundation the Basie band was built upon. Basie had driving, hard-hitting brass and a swinging rhythm section. He created an environment that encouraged growth and allowed individuality to flourish. Many of his players were great soloists, and many went on to careers outside of the Basie band. He was tough when required and conducted his group from the piano bench by gesturing with his eyes, nodding his head, and pointing a finger.

One of the staples of the Basie library is *April in Paris*. The album was recorded in two separate sessions in December 1955 and January 1956, when the band was playing regularly at New York's Birdland. From these dates came three important songs that helped to revitalize the Basie orchestra and in the process became jazz standards.

Vernon Duke's "April in Paris" came from the 1932 musical *Walk a Little Faster*. Basie's version is the most famous, and it climbed to number twenty-eight on the pop charts in 1956. The public loved it, in particular Thad Jones's trumpet's quotes from "Pop Goes the Weasel" and the false ending where Basie says, "One more time." It is this performance of "April in Paris" that was inducted into the Grammy Hall of Fame in 1985.

"Corner Pocket" was co-written by Basie's long-time guitarist Freddie Green. (After Jon Hendricks wrote lyrics to it, it became "Until I Met You.") The song features an arrangement written by Ernie Wilkins that has the trumpets of Thad Jones and Joe Newman coming in strong after a brisk introduction by Basie on piano. Saxophonist Frank Foster's "Shiny Stockings" is a compositional masterpiece, and the band plays it in a hard-blowing jazz mood.

One of the reasons this album is so good is that Basie kept it simple and swinging. He came from the less-is-best school of playing. He could pop the right note when the band was taking a breath. Basie played short lines with his right hand, with occasional punctuations by his left hand, while guitar and bass provided the rhythm functions normally played by the left hand. Freddie Green, on acoustic guitar, was a masterful rhythm guitarist and time-keeper. Drummer Sonny Payne was an innovator who laid out the time with wire brushes on a high-hat cymbal and worked the bass drum softly.

This is great big band music, and *April in Paris* is a high-water mark for Basie and his sixteen-piece orchestra. This is a big band at the top of its game.

■―――

Verve #3145214022

◼

LENNIE TRISTANO, 1919–78
Lennie Tristano
Recorded in New York City, 1955 and 1960–62

Pianist Lennie Tristano was born in Chicago in 1919 at the peak of the influenza pandemic that infected much of the world. The 'flu came close to killing Tristano in his first year but instead it left him blind. His mother, a pianist and opera singer, taught him to play piano, and at a school for the blind in Chicago, he learned music theory. Later, he attended Chicago's American Conservatory of Music before moving to New York City in 1946.

Tristano is an overlooked figure in jazz, partly because his critics thought that his playing was too technical and devoid of emotion. But his fans appreciated the absence of flash in Tristano's style and believed his use of counterpoint (a technique involving the simultaneous playing of separate musical ideas) was ground-breaking. It was. Tristano was a shy man whose experiments with free improvisation were some of the first recorded moments of what later became known as free jazz. He might have been better known if he had concentrated on recording and performing, but instead he devoted his life to teaching.

In 1951, in New York City, he founded one of the first jazz schools. The faculty featured some of his students, including saxophonists Lee Konitz and Warne Marsh. Tristano closed the school in 1956 but continued teaching from his home on Long Island. He loved the early jazz recordings of Louis Armstrong and Lester Young and demanded his students study the important solos so they would learn how improvised solos are constructed and unlearn the poor musical habits they had already developed.

He was an innovative teacher, and his advanced understanding of music theory made him an interesting choice for students. At various times, Phil Woods, Bill Evans, Sheila Jordan, Herbie Hancock, Charles Mingus, Warne Marsh, and Lee Konitz all studied with Tristano. And such artists as Charlie Parker and Bud Powell used his innovations in harmony and counterpoint in their own work.

Two albums he recorded for Atlantic Records, *Lennie Tristano* and *The New Tristano*, are considered important because the music is complex and interesting. They constitute the material on the 1994 release *Lennie Tristano* (Rhino/Warner). The first four selections were recorded in his home studio in 1955. The first song, "Line Up," and the fourth, "East Thirty-Second," are pulsating numbers with Peter Ind on bass and Jeff Morton on drums. Tristano overdubbed several pianos and played with the speed of the tapes. The plaintive ballad "Requiem," the second track, is a beautiful piece written as a tribute to Charlie Parker with just Tristano on piano. The third selection, "Turkish Mambo," has no eastern flavour, but was named as a salute to Ahmet and Neshui Ertegun, co-owners of Atlantic Records. Here, Tristano overdubbed three pianos to achieve the effect he wanted. From a 1955 gig at the Sing Song Room of the Confucius Restaurant in New York come five bewitching standards: "These Foolish Things," "You Go to My Head," "If I Had You," "Ghost of a Chance," and "All the Things You Are," with Lee Konitz on sax, Art Taylor on drums, and Gene Ramey on bass. These are the most conservative tracks on the entire album and provide a glimpse of a more structured, less improvisational side of Tristano.

The remaining six tracks were first recorded on Tristano's 1962 release *The New Tristano*. They are remarkable solo piano improvisations that provide insight into where some of Chick Corea and Keith Jarrett's musical ideas came from.

■ ──

Rhino #71595

■

SONNY ROLLINS, b. 1930
Sonny Rollins: Saxophone Colossus
Recorded in New York City, June 22, 1956

Sonny Rollins is arguably the greatest living improviser in jazz. His muscular, meaty tenor-sax playing and eloquent improvisations have made him an intimidating wonder of jazz.

Rollins is also one of the jazz world's more interesting people. Three times he has taken a sabbatical from music. His initial break in 1954 was his most desperate, as he spent it at the federal drug treatment facility in Lexington, Kentucky, where he kicked his heroin addiction. Afterward, he spent several months in Chicago preparing to re-enter the jazz scene. Then in 1959, frustrated by what he thought were his musical limitations, he took his most famous break from public performing. To spare an expectant mother in his apartment building in New York's Lower East Side the sound of his practising, he took to playing late at night on the pedestrian walkway of the Williamsburg Bridge. When he returned to the jazz scene in 1961, he called his comeback album *The Bridge*. Rollins took his last sabbatical in 1968 to study yoga, meditation, and Eastern philosophies. By the time he returned to the music scene in 1971, he had become more interested in R&B and funk.

Sonny Rollins's successes are as well documented as his failures. In an article about Rollins in the June 2005 issue of *JazzTimes*, seventeen jazz musicians were polled for their favourite Sonny Rollins performances. Only one mentioned a recording after 1966.

His most impressive body of work comes from the years 1956 to 1962 and includes *Saxophone Colossus, Way Out West, Tenor Madness,*

A Night at the Village Vanguard, and *The Bridge.* All demonstrate energy, endurance, and inspiration.

The pivotal recording in bringing about the widespread acceptance of Rollins as a major figure is *Saxophone Colossus.* It inspired critics to write scholarly analyses and fans to revel in the hard-swinging invention, humour, and tender balladry of Rollins's playing. It was recorded in just one day in New York City, while Rollins was still a member of Clifford Brown's group. The contributions of pianist Tommy Flanagan's elegant swing, bassist Doug Watkins's steady lift, and drummer Max Roach's soloing helped make this a landmark album.

The album includes Rollins's best-known composition, "St. Thomas," a Caribbean calypso based on a song his mother sang to him as a child. His rendition of "Moritat" (an instrumental version of "Mack the Knife") smoulders. "You Don't Know What Love Is" is rich and melodic. Roach and Rollins trade licks on the blues-based "Blue 7" and play off of each other beautifully throughout. Rollins's compelling and brilliantly played solo on this song helped define his style as an improviser.

Saxophone Colossus showcases the marriage of intellect, wit, soul, and guts that, from the record's release onward, marked Rollins as a genius of improvised music.

■ ――――――――――――――――――――――――――――――――――

Prestige #PRCD-7079-2

■

DUKE ELLINGTON, 1899–1974
Ellington at Newport 1956
Recorded at the Newport Jazz Festival, Rhode Island, August 1956

Duke Ellington is one of the most important musical figures of the twentieth century. He refused to recognize boundaries of any kind and created a staggering body of work that includes three thousand compositions and two thousand records.

Born in 1899 in Washington, D.C., Edward Kennedy Ellington grew up to be tall, handsome, and a fashion plate who kept every hair in place. He had a sophisticated and elegant manner and a magnetic personality that women of all ages found appealing. He was a loner and kept everyone, except a special few, at arms length. Like many geniuses he was unpredictable.

Ellington kept his band going for fifty years, not out of loyalty but because he liked having an orchestra around to play his new compositions. Thanks to this musical obsession, he left us with many of the most recognizable songs of the twentieth century. He could write anywhere, under almost any circumstance. Once, while on a plane he asked a member of his band if he had any manuscript paper. When Ellington was told no, he took off his suit jacket and wrote in pen on the sleeve of his white shirt the eight bars he had in his head. On the last day of his life in the hospital, he wrote out thirty-two bars on manuscript paper, rolled over, fell asleep, and died.

In the 1940s, Ellington was at the pinnacle of his career, leading an orchestra built around the musicians he had recruited personally. But in the late 1940s, ballrooms were closing, singers started to rule the hit parade, and big bands were breaking up, one by one. The future looked bleak, but Ellington was determined to keep his orchestra going. When the payroll was difficult to meet out of earnings, he would dig into his own pocket and use his composing royalties. By the mid-1950s, Ellington was at a low point. His records weren't selling, some of his players had left, he had placed a distant fourth to Count Basie's band in a *Down Beat* reader's poll, and he had also left Capitol Records with no recording deal in sight.

Ellington's persistent touring during the lean years paid off when a new avenue for exposure opened up, the jazz festival. He was booked to play the third Newport Jazz Festival in July 1956. By then he had signed with Columbia Records and had written a new piece, "Newport Jazz Festival Suite," which would be premiered at the festival. His new label was going to record the concert.

Ellington at Newport 1956 turned out to be the bestselling album of his career. The orchestra's performance almost caused a riot because of the jubilant reaction of the seven thousand watching. There were bursts of wild dancing, and acres of people jumped up, cheering and clapping. The climax of the night was the performance by one of Ellington's favourite musicians, tenor saxophonist Paul Gonsalves. For twenty-seven straight choruses (three and a half minutes) he played the bridge between two of Ellington's compositions, "Diminuendo in Blue" and "Crescendo in Blue." Ellington's career was relaunched.

When the concert was first cut on vinyl, it consisted of the above selections and the closing song, "Jeep's Blues." Because some of the live recording was not up to Columbia's technical standard, and Gonsalves had played into the wrong mic, Ellington and his orchestra went into a New York studio and rerecorded some of the music from that night. When the album was released later that year, it was a cut-and-paste job, with some of the live music from the festival and some from the studio recordings, mixed with fake stage announcements and applause.

The 1999 double-CD edition of the album, *Ellington at Newport 1956*, sets it straight by assembling in sequence the complete live performance as well as the material recorded in the studio for the original release. In total it includes one hundred minutes of previously unreleased music.

Duke led his fifteen men, including a recently returned Johnny Hodges on sax, Harry Carney on baritone sax, Clark Terry and Ray Nance on trumpets, and Sam Woodyard on drums, with gusto and nervy moves, creating a beautiful, careful blending of diverse musical talents that is so stylish, so unique, and so right.

■───

Columbia #CK 40587

SHELLY MANNE, 1920–84
My Fair Lady
Recorded in Los Angeles, August 17, 1956

In the 1950s and 1960s, Sheldon "Shelly" Manne was one of the most in-demand and widely liked jazz drummers in Los Angeles. He devoted so much of his time to the lucrative session scene that his own contribution to jazz is often underappreciated.

Music was part of his life from the day Manne was born, as both his father and uncles were drummers in New York. Manne's first instrument was the saxophone, but when he was eighteen he switched to the drums. In the 1940s, with the exception of a three-year stint in the Coast Guard, Manne played drums in the big bands of Les Brown, Woody Herman, and Stan Kenton. The bebop of Manhattan's 52nd Street appealed to the young drummer, and he played with Dizzy Gillespie and Charlie Parker.

In the early 1950s, Manne and his wife moved from New York to California to live on a ranch outside Los Angeles, where they raised horses while he continued to play. The combination of his good nature and great talent made him a popular choice for both live and studio work. Manne appeared on thousands of albums, including releases by Frank Sinatra, Ella Fitzgerald, Tom Waits, Barry Manilow, Mel Torme, Sarah Vaughan, Shorty Rogers, Art Pepper, and Chet Baker, and made fifteen albums with his own groups. He played on hundreds of film and television soundtracks, including the movies *One From the Heart*, *The Benny Goodman Story*, and *The Gene Krupa Story*, and he instructed Frank Sinatra for the drumming sequence in *The Man With the Golden Arm*. He was a favourite of composers John Williams, André Previn, Jerry

Goldsmith, Quincy Jones, and Henry Mancini. From 1960 to 1974, he co-owned Shelly's Manne-Hole, a jazz club in Hollywood and the location of live jazz albums by Bill Evans, Michel Legrand, and Lenny Breau.

The musical *My Fair Lady* (based on George Bernard Shaw's play *Pygmalion*) opened in New York City on March 15, 1956, and ran for 2,717 performances, setting a record on Broadway. For decades, Broadway musicals were mined by jazz musicians, and to beat the rush of other musical tributes to *My Fair Lady* that were bound to come, Manne quickly recorded his own five months later, in a trio with André Previn on piano and Leroy Vinnegar on bass.

Although *My Fair Lady* is billed as by the Shelly Manne Trio, it is very much a collaboration between Manne and Previn. At the time of the recording, Previn was a bright light in Hollywood music. He was twenty-seven and had recently completed scoring his twenty-fifth film. In 1964, he received an Academy Award for his work on the movie adaptation of *My Fair Lady*. Today he is thought of primarily as a conductor, but in the mid- to late-1950s he also worked as a jazz musician. If jazz had remained his focus, he could have become one of the genre's top pianists.

The trio recorded eight songs from *My Fair Lady*, including "Get Me to the Church On Time," "On the Street Where You Live," "I've Grown Accustomed to Her Face," and "I Could Have Danced All Night." The melodies and harmonies of the original compositions are kept intact. Manne's playing is steady, swinging, and responsive. The whole album is the sound of three consummate professionals who are at the top of their game.

■ ───

Contemporary Records #7527

BOB DOROUGH, b. 1923
Devil May Care
Recorded in New York City, October 1956

Many of Bob Dorough's fans know him not as a jazz musician but as the composer and singer of songs on *Schoolhouse Rock*, a hit children's educational television show in the 1970s and 1980s. As the musical director of the show, Dorough was responsible for many of the series' most popular songs: "Rock Conjunction," "Junction," "Three Is a Magic Number," and "My Hero, Zero."

Dorough was born on December 12, 1923. In person he is warm, engaging, and just a bit eccentric. His accent comes courtesy of his birthplace, Cherry Hill, Arkansas, and time spent living in Texas. He's bald on top but still has enough hair in the back for a ponytail. He has marvellous, infectious enthusiasm and what seems like a perpetual schoolboy grin.

In 1949, Dorough received a degree in music composition from North Texas State University. His passion was jazz, but in those days in Texas, jazz didn't pay the rent. Still, he was able to play music, making money by working at Henry Le Tang's dance studio, accompanying tap dancers on the piano. This led to his meeting boxer Sugar Ray Robinson and becoming his musical director for two years in the early 1950s. In 1954, he moved to Paris and recorded with Blossom Dearie. In 1956, back in the States, he made his first album, *Devil May Care*. Miles Davis became a fan and later recorded three of his songs, two of which Dorough sang ("Blue Xmas" and "Nothing Like You"). In the 1960s, he co-wrote "Comin' Home Baby" for Mel Torme and later worked with the Chad Mitchell Trio, co-producing the hits "Sunday Morning" and "Like to Get to Know You" for the rock band Spanky and Our Gang. He co-wrote "I'm Hip" with his friend David Frishberg. In the nineties, Diana Krall resurrected "Devil May Care."

The song can be found on Dorough's classic first release, *Devil May Care*, made for a small New York independent label, Bethlehem Records. It features Dorough on both piano and vocals. His idiosyncratic voice has a syrupy rasp, as if Nat King Cole were trying to impersonate Louis Armstrong. His piano playing is steady and solid.

In the time leading up to this recording, Dorough was in good form because he had been performing live for three months. The album opens with Dorough scatting along with Warren Fitzgerald's trumpet on the uptempo "Old Devil Moon," before he breaks into the lyrics. Dizzy Gillespie's "Ow" is bebop heaven and is sung wordlessly. Dorough's vocalese tribute to Charlie Parker was written just after he passed away. "Yardbird Suite" features his own lyrics put to the classic jazz number. It was after hearing this song that Miles Davis became a fan.

There is another side to Dorough, warm and sentimental. His version of Hoagy Carmichael's "Baltimore Oriole" is delightful. Dorough's laid-back delivery and horn-like phrasing make it the hippest version ever recorded. Duke Ellington and Billy Strayhorn's 1942 lament to love, "I Don't Mind," is beautifully and convincingly done, and you have to wonder why more singers have not recorded it. The album's most important and popular track is the defiant "Devil May Care." This is the first glimpse of Dorough as a songwriter.

Devil May Care is an album inspired by the vocals of gurus Annie Ross, Eddie Jefferson, and King Pleasure. Dorough's singing incorporates vocalese and scat styles and gives them a friendly and informal nasal delivery. At times he sounds as if he was having problems with pitch and staying in tune but ultimately the flaws are all part of his charm, which is without a doubt, unique in jazz.

■ ———————————————————————————————

Bethlehem #4004

■

THELONIOUS MONK, 1917–82
Brilliant Corners
Recorded in New York City, October–December 1956

Thelonious Sphere Monk's sound owes a great deal to the stride piano style of James P. Johnson, Willie "the Lion" Smith, and Duke Ellington. Monk didn't compose a large body of work, just sixty to seventy songs in all, but today many of them are jazz standards, including "Ruby My Dear," "Well You Needn't," "Pannonica," "Straight, No Chaser," and "'Round Midnight." The last being one of the most recorded songs in jazz.

Monk was an original in many aspects of his life: his fashion sense, his speech, appearance, and behaviour. He was hospitalized several times for an undetermined mental illness that grew worse in the late 1960s.

Monk's uniqueness was most apparent in the complicated sound of his music. His strange melodies and unusual harmonics led the jazz critic Whitney Balliett to describe them as bouncing "with dissonances and rhythms that often give one the sensation of missing the bottom step in the dark."

In the late 1930s and early 1940s, Monk was the pianist in the house band at Minton's Playhouse in Harlem, where other unknowns, such as Dizzy Gillespie and Charlie Parker, came to play. Collectively they helped create a new style of jazz called bebop.

Monk's first big break came in the early 1940s when pianist Bud Powell convinced Cootie Williams, in whose orchestra he was playing, to record "'Round Midnight." Williams took co-writer credit, although he did not collaborate on the composition. Monk made his first recording as a leader in 1947 for Blue Note.

In 1951, Monk was busted for narcotics and stripped of his cabaret card, which made it impossible for him to play the clubs of New York City. Monk was largely ignored in jazz until producer Orrin Keepnews paid out his contract at Prestige Records for $108.27 in 1955 and set up his own label, Riverside Records. He then signed Monk, and through several carefully made albums helped him claim the jazz real-estate he deserved.

Monk's third album for Riverside, *Brilliant Corners*, is a masterpiece. The band doing most of the heavy lifting makes beautiful, rambunctious music and features Sonny Rollins on sax, Oscar Pettiford on bass, Max Roach on drums, and Monk on piano. The title song, "Brilliant Corners," is so nervy and difficult to play that after twenty-five attempts, Monk stopped recording it. The final piece on the album, the song consists of various takes spliced together.

Monk possessed one of the must unique sounds in jazz. "Balue Bolivar Ba-lues-are" is a blues song with a great rhythmic sparkle. The title refers to the Hotel Bolivar in Manhattan, then the home of his friend Baroness Pannonica "Nica" de Koenigswarter. Another of the album's standout tracks is the beautiful ballad "Pannonica," which features Monk doubling on celeste. It is another of his tributes to the baroness, whom he met in Paris in 1954. Until the day he died, she was his patron and biggest supporter. He spent the last ten years of his life living in the baroness's mansion in Weehawken, New Jersey.

Brilliant Corners remains a strong musical announcement that displays Monk's compositional genius, his passion and brilliance. While many musicians struggled throughout their careers to find a strong musical identity, Monk found his own voice and, despite much ridicule, carved out his place in jazz. *Brilliant Corners* laid the foundation.

■ ───────────────────────────────────

Riverside #RLP12-226

ELLA FITZGERALD AND LOUIS ARMSTRONG
The Complete Ella Fitzgerald and Louis Armstrong on Verve
Recorded in Los Angeles, 1956–57

The idea of recording two of the giants of jazz, Ella Fitzgerald and Louis Armstrong, as a duo, in 1956 was absolutely brilliant. Fitzgerald was the first lady of song and blessed with a refined, beautiful voice and wide range. Armstrong was the creator of jazz singing, and his charming, freewheeling voice was one of the most recognizable in the world. The musical genius behind their collaboration was Norman Granz, the founder of Verve Records, who produced their three albums.

In 1997, all the tracks Ella and Louis recorded for Verve Records were reissued as a three-CD set called *The Complete Ella Fitzgerald and Louis Armstrong on Verve*. Discs one and two are the legendary LPs *Ella and Louis* and *Ella and Louis Again*, on which they were backed by an all-star house band: Oscar Peterson, Ray Brown, Louis Bellson, and Buddy Rich. Disc three is Gershwin's *Porgy and Bess*, featuring orchestrations by Russ Garcia.

All forty-seven songs were recorded in Los Angeles between 1956 and 1957. Logistics were a problem. While Fitzgerald lived in Los Angeles, she toured extensively, and Armstrong was based in New York City but was a virtual road warrior because of his non-stop touring. The sessions, a day here and a day there, were scheduled around Armstrong's limited availability.

For their repertoire, Fitzgerald and Armstrong had for their use the entire songbook of American popular music. Granz was a strong believer in its commercial appeal and selected for them songs by many of the greats, including Irving Berlin, George Gershwin, Cole Porter, Harold Arlen, and Hoagy Carmichael.

The contrast between their voices is one of the album's biggest charms. Their duets on "They Can't Take That Away From Me," "Let's Call the Whole Thing Off," "I Won't Dance," and "The Nearness of You" are some of the most extraordinary moments in jazz. Other than knowing in advance what songs Granz had selected, Fitzgerald and Armstrong had no preparation before recording. In the studio, some adjustments were made to certain selections to accommodate the key and range of each singer. To so quickly achieve the warmth and ease on these recordings is a testament to the musical brilliance and consummate professionalism of the two.

On certain selections there is an opportunity for each to shine without the other. Armstrong's bluesy, growly delivery of "Let's Do It" is a gem. At 8:44, it provides Armstrong plenty of time to stretch out on vocals and trumpet. Fitzgerald's swinging version of "Comes Love" showcases a singer with phenomenal technique and impeccable timing.

One composer's name that turns up frequently here is George Gershwin, in particular on the third disc of the music for his opera *Porgy and Bess*. It is a huge departure from the intimate sound of the first two CDs. Russ Garcia's big and powerful arrangements are over the top, but the opera is a beautiful concept for Fitzgerald and Armstrong to record. Their duets on "Bess, You Is My Woman Now," "Summertime," and "It Ain't Necessarily So" are glorious.

The Complete Ella Fitzgerald and Louis Armstrong on Verve is an extraordinary work from two of the most important contributors to jazz.

■ —————————————————————————————————

Verve #3145372842

MOSE ALLISON, b. 1927
Allison Wonderland
Recorded in New York, Los Angeles, and New Orleans, 1957–91

Listening to Mose Allison's music properly is an exercise in alertness. He draws on jazz, R&B, and country music to come up with his sound. Lyrically, he has the intellectual flair of a beat poet and satirist combined. His voice sounds southern, hip, and uncomplicated.

Allison has fans around the world, but in Britain it was rock bands that first embraced his satirical music. Over the years, his songs have been recorded by the Yardbirds, John Mayall, Elvis Costello, the Clash, Robert Palmer, Eric Clapton, Brian Auger, the Who, and Van Morrison. In North America you can find versions of his songs by Diana Krall, Colin James, Johnny Winter, the Kingston Trio, John Hammond, and Bonnie Raitt.

There are many influences in Allison's playing: bluesman Percy Mayfield figures prominently; there is even a hint of Muddy Waters, Tampa Red, and Sonny Boy Williamson. Not surprisingly, some of his new fans, without seeing him, assume he is black. In the 1960s, while he was playing Chicago, *Jet* magazine tracked him down and proposed doing a story on him. Allison explained to the writer there was something the magazine should know.

Allison and his trio first played instrumental music, but lyrics quickly found their way into his repertoire. He has said that for every person who understands music there are five hundred who understand words. His lyrics have a kind of southern pessimism and yet a strong understanding of the human condition. An irony, if you will.

Allison Wonderland is a career-defining double-CD retrospec-. tive. There are forty-six songs from five different labels spanning the years from 1957 to 1991.

Allison's best-known song, "Back Country Blues" (a.k.a. "Young Man's Blues"), is a scathing, timeless piece about oppression and lack of opportunity in an older person's world. The Who turned it into a youth anthem when the song appeared on their *Live at Leeds* album. Allison recorded it in 1957, and it appeared on his first album, *Back Country Suite for Piano, Bass and Drums*.

Another song from 1957 is "Parchman Farm," a bit of fiction about being imprisoned in the Mississippi State Penitentiary in Parchman, which Allison lived near as a child. It is a tongue-in-cheek song Allison seldom performs today because of its unfortunate gag line, "All I did was shoot my wife."

"Your Mind Is on Vacation" is Allison's second best-known song. He has recorded it several times, but this version from 1962 is the original. It was written as a put-down of smug know-it-alls. Allison decided it was a good song when he realized it applied to him.

"Stop This World" is a perfect example of Allison at his darkest and most despondent. The unflinching honesty of this song made it a favourite of many performers after 9/11.

"Top 40" is Allison's scornful and biting look at the recording industry and its formula for success. As he puts it, all you need is a dynamite, freaked-out, solid-gold, top-forty, big-beat, rock-and-roll record.

His music is often thought of as being comical. It certainly has humorous ingredients, but it is also very profound. With forty-seven songs on this retrospective, Allison's one-two punch on the world is felt strongly. His songs have a poignancy and substance that will keep them relevant for years to come.

Rhino #71689

■

NINA SIMONE, 1933–2003
Jazz as Played in an Exclusive Side Street Club
Recorded in New York City, 1957

In 1954, a young classically trained pianist named Eunice Wayman took a job playing piano at the seedy Midtown Bar and Grill in Atlantic City, New Jersey. To hide the gig from her opinionated mother, a Methodist minister, Wayman adopted another name: Nina Simone. She took Nina (meaning "girl" or "little one" in Spanish) from a pet name that a boyfriend had given her and Simone from the French actress Simone Signoret.

Nina Simone was an artist of enormous depth and influence. Black classical music was how she categorized her sound, which blended African rhythms, folk, blues, and gospel with jazz. Simone launched her career in the 1950s, a time when the music world was dominated by uncompromising men. She was outspoken about civil rights issues and contributed several important songs to the movement, including her scathing "Mississippi Goddam," which was written in response to the death of four black children in a church bombing, and "Young, Gifted and Black," which became an anthem for African Americans in the 1960s and 1970s.

From time to time, Simone hurt her career with much publicized outbursts of temper and sometimes bewildering changes in mood. There were concerts where she failed to show up. Her relationship with record companies was turbulent, with periods of no recording. After a disagreement with the IRS over unpaid taxes, she became disillusioned with life in the United States, and in 1974 she moved to Barbados. In the following years, she lived in Liberia, Switzerland, Paris, and the Netherlands before retiring to the south of France, where she lived until her death in 2003.

Some of the songs Simone played at the Midtown Bar can be found on her first album, *Jazz as Played in an Exclusive Side Street Club* (sometimes called *Little Girl Blue*). It was recorded in 1957 for the small independent label Bethlehem Records. Simone and her band, including Jimmy Bond on bass and Albert "Tootie" Heath on drums, recorded for fourteen hours straight.

Simone's original plan was to be the first black concert pianist, and "Love Me or Leave" shows her making good use of her Juilliard training by incorporating Bach for a couple of choruses. Her version of Rodgers and Hart's "Little Girl Blue," in which she uses the melody of "Good King Wenceslas" as a counterpoint, is ingenious.

The marvellous, low-key intensity she brought to Gershwin's "I Loves You, Porgy" earned her her first hit. Although Simone recorded the song several times over her career, this is the first and defining version.

Simone's sensitive, heart-on-her-sleeve interpretation of ballads was one of her major strengths as a performer. She's in top soulful form on the atmospheric "Don't Smoke in Bed," which was a hit for Peggy Lee in 1948.

"My Baby Just Cares for Me," the best-known song on the album, was an afterthought. Simone's producer decided that an extra uptempo song was needed to help balance the number of ballads that had been recorded. In 1987, thirty years after it was first released, the song was used as the theme for a British television commercial for the perfume Chanel No. 5. Released as a single not long afterward, it sold 175,000 copies in the first week, making it a number-five chart hit in the U.K. Charly, the British label that licensed the material from Bethlehem, was not required to pay her, but allegedly offered $20,000 in royalties.

Nina Simone's life was a long and intense journey, but along the way she created much beautiful music.

Bethlehem, #6028

MILES DAVIS, 1926–91
Miles Ahead
Recorded in New York City, May–August 1957

When Miles Davis signed with Columbia Records, he knew he had joined the ranks of an illustrious recording roster that included Leopold Stokowski, Leonard Bernstein, and Benny Goodman. He had also moved to a large label that had the resources to realize projects on a grand scale.

Davis's first big project for Columbia was an orchestral album, *Miles Ahead*. The idea was staff producer George Avakian's, who explained it over lunch one day to Davis and his friend, arranger Gil Evans. Avakian had been impressed by the nonet material Davis had recorded in the 1940s and wanted to expand the concept to a nineteen-piece orchestra. The two could choose the music as long as Davis gave Avakian an original song called "Miles Ahead," so Columbia could develop a marketing campaign based on the idea that Miles was ahead of everyone else.

Davis was notoriously prickly to work with and cautious with almost everyone, but Evans was the exception. Evans was fourteen years Davis's senior and had his unconditional musical trust; the two remained best friends until Evans died in 1988. As the album started to take shape, Evans chose all the music except for two songs provided by Davis: "New Rhumba," which was written by Ahmad Jamal, and "The Duke," by Dave Brubeck. Evans's choices included Kurt Weill's "My Ship," Bobby Troup's "The Meaning of the Blues," and J.J. Johnson's "Lament."

Although credited as a Miles Davis album, *Miles Ahead* is very much a collaboration with Evans, whose role as the arranger was almost equal to Davis's. Evans was paid five hundred dollars a song for arranging the album but received no royalties on sales. He recomposed the songs, often altering the melody line or changing the tempo, and decided how and what instruments would be used. The Evans sound relied heavily on French horns and tuba, as well as traditional jazz instrumentation, with almost no soloing and a preference for ensemble playing. He was a perfectionist who made the orchestra rehearse the pieces numerous times and asked for multiple takes to be recorded so often that several of the musicians complained of playing fatigued. Avakian, sensing he might not get what he needed, recorded everything that was happening in the studio as a precaution. Years later, he explained that the recordings were extensively edited for the finished album. Davis was comfortable with the concept of music editing and continued to make full use of the opportunities it provided for the rest of his career.

For Davis, *Miles Ahead* was a departure of sorts; instead of playing his trumpet, he used the flugelhorn, which is similar but has a mellower and darker sound. Davis's playing is stark and mournful, floating lyrically above the songs, particularly on the delicate ballads.

Miles Ahead is a masterpiece, a monument in the history of jazz.

∎

Sony BMG #CK 65121

JIMMY SMITH, 1925–2005
The Sermon
Recorded in New York City, August 1957 and February 1958

Jimmy Smith playing his Hammond B3 organ was a remarkable sight. As he moved his feet over the bass pedals, hammered chords with his left hand, and hovered over the high notes with his right, he made a jubilant sound that blended jazz, blues, rhythm and blues, bebop, and even gospel into an exhilarating stew that became known as soul jazz or funk.

Born in Norristown, Pennsylvania, Smith first learned piano and studied at the Orstein School of Music in Philadelphia. In 1951, he switched to the Hammond B3 and soon attracted a following. Although he wasn't the first jazz musician to play the organ, he was the man who took it out of the church and theatre and permanently put it in the jazz club. He was the first to break ground with the instrument in a career that spanned five decades. His accomplishments are all the more remarkable when you consider that he didn't start playing the organ until he was twenty-seven.

As Smith's career progressed, his sound became formulaic and routine, but his work in the late 1950s and early 1960s was exciting, and many of his best albums are from this period, on Blue Note. He recorded thirty in total for the label, from his 1956 *New Sounds on the Organ* to 1963, when he left the label for Verve. He recorded in a variety of settings at Blue Note and worked with some of the major players of the day, including guitarist Kenny Burrell, trumpet player Lee Morgan, and sax players Lou Donaldson, Tina Brooks, Jackie McLean, Ike Quebec, and Stanley Turrentine.

His finest recording for the label was 1958's *The Sermon*. On paper, it looks as if it was doomed to fail. It's an album with just three tracks – the longest of which exceeds twenty minutes – featuring the Hammond B3 organ, which until then was most often thought of as a novelty instrument played at roller rinks. Yet everything about it works.

The Sermon delivers a steady stream of soul jazz, with repeated hooks and big, fat, greasy chords. The title song, a twelve-bar blues, was Smith's tribute to one of his Blue Note label mates, pianist Horace Silver. The groove is locked in by Smith and builds slowly, solo after solo.

First a solid foundation is laid down by Art Blakey on drums, as Smith preaches with a down-home sound, and then Kenny Burrell comes in with a soulful guitar solo, Tina Brooks steps in to wail on tenor sax, and Lee Morgan plays a rich solo on trumpet. Blue Note regular Lou Donaldson carries the next solo on alto sax, and lastly Smith brings it home.

"J.O.S." is from an earlier session done in the summer of 1957. It is a raw, blues-based potboiler, with appearances by soloists George Coleman on alto sax and Lee Morgan on trumpet. Smith has a funky presence that punctuates the song.

On the last selection, Burrell, Morgan, and Blakey return for a version of the beautiful "Flamingo." Morgan plays the main solo on trumpet. His sound is open and warm; Smith lays down a nice bed to walk on.

Master of the Hammond, Jimmy Smith had many imitators, followers, and fans, and anyone today who plays jazz on the organ is a direct descendant of Smith. He was the first to develop a jazz vocabulary on the instrument.

■ ──

Blue Note #24541

THELONIOUS MONK
Thelonious Monk Quartet with John Coltrane at
Carnegie Hall
Recorded in New York City, November 29, 1957

Whoever first uttered the phrase "Everything old is new again" just might have worked in the music business. The most discussed jazz release in the fall of 2005 was a historic recording made in 1957 featuring pianist Thelonious Monk and tenor saxophonist John Coltrane. For jazz fans, the short six-month collaboration between these two architects of bebop is sacred ground. Once these tapes were found, Sony BMG, Verve, and Blue Note all bid for the rights to release the album. Blue Note won.

On November 29, 1957, Monk and Coltrane performed a benefit at Carnegie Hall for a community centre in Harlem. The concert was professionally recorded by Voice of America for broadcast overseas. After the show, the tapes were poorly labelled, filed in Voice of America's substantial collection of recordings, and soon forgotten. In January 2005, Larry Appelbaum, an engineer and jazz specialist at the Library of Congress, happened upon them when he was digitally transferring the library's collection for preservation purposes.

In early 1957, Coltrane was in crisis. He had been taken from relative obscurity two years earlier when Miles Davis selected him to be a member of his group, but Coltrane's heroin addiction was interfering with his performance. In April 1957, Davis finally fired him because of his inconsistent ways. In May, Coltrane kicked his habit and replaced heroin with spirituality. Coltrane often said this was a pivotal time for him, a creative awakening of sorts. Coltrane started rehearsing with Thelonious Monk and eventually joined his quartet.

In 1957, the musical landscape was good for Monk. People were now lining up around the block in New York to hear him play. His cabaret card, which allowed him to play in clubs, had been returned to him, after being revoked when he was arrested for narcotics possession in 1951.

Monk and Coltrane were four months into their partnership when they stepped on to the stage at Carnegie Hall that night in November. It is obvious from listening to the recording that something very special was taking place. Coltrane had once described playing Monk's music as the equivalent of stepping into an elevator shaft. But by the time of the concert, Coltrane had absorbed the music and was ready to play as Monk's equal. They were one another's support team, displaying fearsome chops and musical brawn.

The nine tracks on this CD include the superlative "Monk's Mood," "Evidence," "Crepuscule with Nellie," and "Blue Monk." Throughout, Monk and Coltrane are daring and innovative and shadow one another effortlessly. This group, which included Shadow Wilson on drums and Ahmed Abdul-Malik on bass, is swinging and adventurous.

Thelonious Monk Quartet with John Coltrane at Carnegie Hall is one of those historic recordings that lives up to its hype.

■ ───────────────────────────────────

Blue Note #35173

BILLIE HOLIDAY, 1915–59
Lady in Satin
Recorded in New York City, February 1958

Considering the events surrounding the recording of *Lady in Satin*, the album should have been a disaster.

Billie Holiday asked Ray Ellis, an unimaginative, middle-of-the-road conductor, to write the arrangements for the album. She then missed all the rehearsals with Ellis, which meant he had to buy copies of her past albums so he could learn the best key for her musical arrangements. His arrangements were syrupy, and the forty-piece orchestra he hired to play them intimidated Holiday. She arrived at the studio stoned and kept her vocal chords lubricated throughout the recording sessions by drinking gin. She hadn't memorized some of the songs she was to record and had to learn the lyrics on the spot. On the last day of recording, she was short one song to complete the album, so a quick trip was made to a nearby music store to find the sheet music for an appropriate song.

The finished product features a once-glorious voice ravaged from years of abuse and hard living. She sounds just plain worn out. But, despite that, *Lady in Satin* stands as a testament to Holiday's genius as a singer and is her greatest and most revealing recording. Although no one realized it at the time, the songs Holiday selected tell a sad story about her life. The theme is unrequited love and the album includes "I'm a Fool to Want You," "You Don't Know What Love Is," "The End of a Love Affair," and "I Get Along Without You Very Well." Her vocal imperfections translated magnificently into the sound of pain and courage. She delivered a performance so commanding it can bring one to tears. Billie Holiday was the ultimate song stylist.

Holiday lived for only another seventeen months after completing this recording.

■—————————————————————————————

Columbia #CK 65144

MICHEL LEGRAND, b. 1932
Legrand Jazz
Recorded in New York City, June 25–30, 1958

Michel Legrand's musical credentials are truly staggering. He has composed more than two hundred film and television scores and several for musicals and has been awarded five Grammys, three Oscars, and an Emmy. His songs include "What Are You Doing the Rest of Your Life?," "The Windmills of Your Mind," and "You Must Believe in Spring," and his body of work has provided the jazz world with a savoury portion of the repertoire musicians rely on to play. His songs have appeared on more than fifteen hundred albums and have been recorded by many of the music world's best, including Frank Sinatra, Bill Evans, Oscar Peterson, Jane Bunnett, Toots Thielemans, and Miles Davis.

Legrand has been associated with pop and film music so often that his skills as a jazz musician are often ignored. Many of his jazz releases are extraordinary recordings that showcase his considerable piano chops and ability to attract the best players.

Legrand was born in Paris in 1932. He was a loner as a child and to stave off boredom he started playing the piano. When he was ten he entered the Paris Conservatory of Music and studied with the great Nadia Boulanger. During the Second World War, jazz was prohibited by the Germans occupying France, but after the war, in 1947, Legrand attended his first jazz concert. Dizzy Gillespie performed two shows in Paris, and Legrand was there for both of them. That was the beginning of his jazz life, and he started buying records by Kenton, Davis, and Basie.

Legrand was twenty-six when he recorded *Legrand Jazz* in 1958. Although he doesn't play on the album, he led the sessions and his musical personality is felt throughout. As the arranger, Legrand adapted eleven famous jazz compositions and selected the musicians to play the songs. Much the way a director casts actors for a play or a painter uses colours, an arranger uses an instrument's sound and a particular musician's approach to playing it to develop an aural painting.

Legrand was also the conductor for this album. He knew the music inside out and back to front and shaped the music the orchestra plays. The musicians are so phenomenal it is hard to believe they were assembled to play on one album. They included Miles Davis, John Coltrane, Bill Evans, Ben Webster, Herbie Mann, and Phil Woods. Having so many high-profile musicians, in particular Miles Davis, caused Legrand some anxiety. He had been told by Miles's friends that if he didn't like what he heard, Miles would walk out of the session. Legrand later said, "I was twenty-four years old, and I was so scared I started sweating. I started to rehearse the orchestra. The door opens, and Miles listens at the door for five minutes. Then he sits down, opens his case and starts to play." In a complete twist of Legrand's expectations, after the first take, Miles wanted to know if the conductor was happy with his playing.

Legrand's decision about which notes are to be played by each instrument is brilliant. The blending of Miles Davis's restrained trumpet with Betty Gramann's delicate harp on "Django" is not only innovative, it is sumptuous. Ben Webster's soulful tenor sax sliding in and out of a four-piece trombone section on "Blue and Sentimental" is inspiring. His use of four great trumpet players on Dizzy Gillespie's bebop anthem "Night in Tunisia" is daring and dazzling. Lastly, Phil Woods's full-bodied alto-sax solo on the Benny Goodman classic "Stompin' at the Savoy" is fearless.

■

Mercury #8300742

ART BLAKEY, 1919–90, AND THE JAZZ MESSENGERS
Moanin'
Recorded in Hackensack, New Jersey, October 1958

Art Blakey was a dynamic leader and a volcanic drummer whose hard-bop band, the Jazz Messengers, was a finishing school for young jazz musicians for almost forty years. His graduates include Hank Mobley, Chuck Mangione, Wayne Shorter, Branford Marsalis, Kenny Dorham, Freddie Hubbard, Wynton Marsalis, Benny Green, Geoff Keezer, John Hicks, Mulgrew Miller, Terence Blanchard, Horace Silver, Cedar Walton, and Keith Jarrett.

Blakey apprenticed in the big bands of the 1940s with Billy Eckstine and Fletcher Henderson, and it was while he was on the road with Fletcher Henderson's group that he survived a beating that left him with a metal plate in his skull. He later played with clarinetist Buddy Defranco and worked as a session drummer, appearing on recordings by Thelonious Monk and Sonny Rollins.

In 1953, Blakey and pianist Horace Silver formed a co-operative band they called the Jazz Messengers, a group that continued in different editions until Blakey's death in 1990. (Silver quit in 1956.)

Art Blakey and the Jazz Messengers were a swinging, energetic force that played hard bop. (The successor to bebop, hard bop has a more intense, driving rhythm.) Blakey sat at the back of the band at his drum kit and laid down a persistent, strong backbeat while he carefully scrutinized the musicians in the front line. Most drummers at the time relied on the bass or kick drum to keep time; Blakey shifted that role to the snare drum and cymbals.

The group was an incubator for young talent, and Blakey taught his musicians how to swing, how to be leaders, about life on the road, and encouraged them to bring in their songs. This resulted in an ever-evolving sound, and each version of the band has its own musical identity. Many of the Jazz Messengers' recordings from the 1950s helped to define Blue Note as a hard bop label.

In 1958, Blakey was leading the third edition of the Jazz Messengers with Lee Morgan on trumpet, Benny Golson on sax, Bobby Timmons on piano, and Jaymie Merritt on bass. In a one-day session on October 30, 1958, they recorded a monumental, free-wheeling album they called *Moanin'*.

Much of the sonic shape of the album can be attributed to Blakey's tenor saxophonist and musical director, Benny Golson, who would go on to become a noted jazz composer. His infectious "Blues March" has the spirit of a New Orleans marching band. "Along Came Betty" was inspired by the walk of the woman it was named after. The melody has a mid-tempo gait and is highlighted at the start by both horns (Golson and Morgan) playing in unison. "The Drum Thunder Suite" is another song written by Golson. The three-part suite showcases Blakey on mallets and brushes.

The standout, hit track from the album is Bobby Timmons's funky classic "Moanin'." It is a well-proportioned tune that uses call and response to reinforce the melody. Timmons's playing is exuberant and fresh. His young age of twenty-two belies the full scope of his talent. This is just as true for twenty-year-old Lee Morgan, who was becoming an increasingly important part of the hard bop Blue Note sound.

The momentum to drive this musical engine comes from Art Blakey. His flawless timing and his energy on the drums is unrelenting and inspiring.

■ ───

Blue Note #95324

RAY CHARLES, 1930–2004
The Genius of Ray Charles
Recorded in New York City, 1959

Ray Charles is one of the most important artists of the twentieth century. His importance is not reflected by his record sales, but by the influence he had on the influencers in music. He was an inspirational artist, not only as a pianist, but also as an arranger, vocalist, and bandleader. He mastered many musical genres – rhythm and blues, country, pop, blues, and jazz – and by combining them, he helped to obliterate musical boundaries. He was the first true crossover artist.

Charles's musical presence was so powerful and distinctive that he is one of the few who could take a song and make it his, even after it had been a hit for someone else. His accomplishments are all the more impressive given the sadness in his life. Born Ray Charles Robinson, into extreme poverty in Albany, Georgia, he experienced an absentee father, his brother's accidental drowning, blindness at age six, racial discrimination, and being orphaned when he was fifteen. Music was his salvation. He took to the music of singers Nat King Cole, Louis Jordan, Charles Brown, and Percy Mayfield, and they continued to influence his music to the end.

Charles's creativity blossomed at an early age, and many of his most artistically important recordings were made for Atlantic Records between 1952 and 1959, while he was in his twenties.

The Genius of Ray Charles was recorded in 1959, when Charles was just twenty-seven, and the album stands as his most musically ambitious recording for the label. It is a collection of twelve standards. Charles had several ideas for the album, including the use of strings. He had grown up listening to the music of big bands, and many of his favourite recordings by singers used string arrangements. He also wanted to sing songs people did not associate with him.

The big band sounds make up the first six tracks of the album, played by musicians from the Ellington and Basie bands, including trumpeter Clark Terry, Paul Gonsalves on tenor sax, guitarist Freddie Green, trumpeter Joe Newman, alto sax player Marshall Royal, as well as Bob Brookmeyer on trombone and Zoot Sims on tenor sax. Charles also made sure that the members of his band, Marcus Belgrave, John Hunt, Edgar Willis, Hank Crawford, and David "Fathead" Newman, were also on the date.

The recording kicks off with a tribute to one of Charles's early influences, Louis Jordan. Jordan recorded the classic swing tune "Let the Good Times Roll" in 1946, when Charles was just sixteen. As soon as Charles yells "Y'all tell everybody Ray Charles is in town," you know that he means business. Charles's friend Quincy Jones wrote an explosive big band arrangement featuring David "Fathead" Newman on tenor sax and with Ray setting the groove and tempo on piano.

Basie alumnus Ernie Wilkins keeps it going with a swinging arrangement of "'Deed I Do." Ralph Burns, of Woody Herman's band, arranged Irving Berlin's "Alexander's Ragtime Band." Burns resurrects this old warhorse of a song in a testament to Charles's brilliance as both a pianist and singer and makes it sound vital and important. Charles surprises and delights with three more big band songs, including "Two Years of Torture," "When Your Lover Has Gone," and "'Deed I Do."

The most revealing songs are the ballads arranged by Ralph Burns and sung with a string orchestra. Charles had heard the work Burns had done for an album by Chris Connor and asked Burns to contribute to his. Highlights include Lil Armstrong's (Satchmo's ex-wife) "Just for a Thrill," another Louis Jordan hit from 1946, "Don't Let the Sun Catch You Crying," and the Harold Arlen and

Johnny Mercer classic "Come Rain or Come Shine." The album is a strong departure from the rhythm and blues and small combo jazz Charles had recorded previously.

In someone else's hands, the sentimentality of the ballads might be a bit much to take, but in Charles's hands they are worth pausing over because he surrenders to the music. He emerges as a warm and sensitive singer who allows us a glimpse into his sad and hurt soul.

■───

Atlantic #1312

◧

MILES DAVIS, 1926–91
Kind of Blue
Recorded in New York City, March–April 1959

Miles Davis was a brilliant musician and an erratic person who made provocative, cavalier statements to the press about race and music. He paid close attention to style and wore the latest fashions and drove expensive cars. He didn't mind being noticed, yet on stage he could be distant and aloof. Davis often played his trumpet with his back to the audience and walked off stage while others soloed. This unusual behaviour was sometimes interpreted as being rude, but Davis wanted the audience to pay attention to his sidemen and not be distracted by his presence.

Davis's music was highly collaborative. He encouraged his musicians to find their voice and, in the process, was inspired by their musical discoveries. In the spring of 1959, Miles and six of his musicians got together in a converted church on 30th Street in Manhattan and made jazz history. *Kind of Blue* is the one album jazz critics consistently agree is *the* essential CD to have in your collection.

As Bill Evans wrote in the original liner notes, "Miles conceived these settings only hours before the recording dates and arrived with sketches which indicated what was to be played." It has been reported that the ideas were written by Davis on scraps of paper in the back seat of a cab en route to the studio.

The creative heart of the album was based on "modal" jazz, an approach to playing music developed by the pianist and jazz theorist George Russell. In his liner notes for the 1997 reissue of *Kind of Blue*, music critic Robert Palmer describes modal jazz as the sound that arrived when "the improviser was given a scale or series of scales as material to improvise from, rather than a sequence of chords or harmonies."

Prior to *Kind of Blue*, Davis felt jazz had become thick, with too many chords to play. He was interested in melody, brevity, and sparseness. For him, music was not only which notes were played but also which were not played and how the space between notes is used. This was the novel approach that Davis brought to *Kind of Blue*. The result is a jazz masterpiece. It is the source of several of the most popular compositions in jazz today, including "Freddie Freeloader," "All Blues," and "So What." The musicians, including Davis on trumpet, Jimmy Cobb on drums, Bill Evans and Wynton Kelly on piano, John Coltrane and Cannonball Adderley on saxophone, and Paul Chambers on bass, play line after line of warm, inspired beauty. It's no wonder that this is the best-selling jazz album of all time.

■ ───

Columbia #CK 64935

JOHN COLTRANE, 1926–67
Giant Steps
Recorded in New York City, April–December 1959

John Coltrane is one of the two most accomplished saxophonists in the history of jazz, the other being Charlie Parker. Coltrane blazed new sonic trails on his alto sax in songs that still sound fresh and timeless. He wrote and recorded numerous masterpieces, such as "Giant Steps," "Naima," "Central Park West," and "A Love Supreme," and brilliantly arranged the Broadway hit "My Favourite Things," transforming it into a standard part of the jazz repertoire. He also made a significant contribution to the sound of *Kind of Blue*, Miles Davis's pivotal release.

From the mid- to late-1950s, there were three key developments in Coltrane's career. The first was when Coltrane apprenticed with Davis in 1955–56. Davis was fond of Coltrane's sound and in particular loved how he could play the five notes of a chord and keep changing them around, in endlessly inventive ways. Miles was also a tough critic and, during one gig, asked Coltrane why his solos lasted so long. Coltrane innocently explained that he didn't know how to stop. Davis teasingly suggested that he just take the saxophone out of his mouth. This was a difficult time for Coltrane – his life was in crisis; Davis eventually fired him because of his narcotics use.

At the start of 1958, after kicking his heroin addiction, Coltrane was back with Davis. In 1959, he played on the famous *Kind of Blue* record. It was a seminal album because most jazz until then had largely featured fast-moving changes. The *Kind of Blue* songs were more relaxed, and the musicians played short musical vamps, using them as the foundation for improvisation.

Kind of Blue gave Coltrane the creative impetus to record his next project, *Giant Steps*, his first album for Atlantic. Just two weeks later, Coltrane was in the studio with the same drummer, Jimmy Cobb, and bassist, Paul Chambers, used by Davis. An extraordinary year in jazz, 1959 saw four pivotal albums recorded in New York City: *Giant Steps*; *Kind of Blue*; *Mingus Ah Um* by Charles Mingus; and *Time Out* by the Dave Brubeck Quartet.

Giant Steps was just that. It represented Coltrane's arrival as both a composer and a soloist. Most of the songs took shape when he was rehearsing at home, and his family plays a prominent role in the album. "Naima" is a loving, tender tribute to his wife. Coltrane's playing here is beautifully sorrowful, and the song remains one of his most emotional melodic compositions. "Syeeda's Song Flute" is named for Coltrane's ten-year-old daughter. It reminded him of her because it sounded happy. The blues-flavoured "Cousin Mary" was a tribute to his cousin Mary Alexander, whom he grew up with in North Carolina.

The album's title song, "Giant Steps," gets its name because of Paul Chambers's loping bass line. Tommy Flanagan's frugal piano solo and his use of space are a magnificent contrast to the fast-paced note clusters Coltrane plays.

The seven songs that comprise *Giant Steps* helped open new doors for Coltrane. There were new possibilities for improvisation, and the album signalled just how far he was going to go beyond the boundaries of contemporary jazz.

Rhino #75203

LAMBERT, HENDRICKS & ROSS
(Dave Lambert, 1917–66, Jon Hendricks,
b. 1921, and Annie Ross, b. 1930)
The Hottest New Group in Jazz
Recorded in New York City, 1959 and 1960, and Chicago, 1961

Long before the vocal gymnastics of the Manhattan Transfer
and Bobby McFerrin attracted attention, there was Lambert,
Hendricks & Ross: Dave Lambert, Jon Hendricks, and Annie
Ross. Granted, their names sound more like a law firm than a vocal
group, but decades after their demise, LH&R remain the hippest
and most innovative vocal stylists in jazz. Their gift to jazz was a
distinct musical identity, a style of singing called vocalese, which
sounds as natural as breathing. Vocalese starts with the setting of
lyrics to jazz orchestra instrumentals, then the voices are arranged
and substituted for an instrument or even a section of instruments.

The trio came together during jam sessions held in Dave
Lambert's New York apartment. He was an arranger and singer who
had sung with bandleaders Gene Krupa, Buddy Stewart, and
Charlie Parker. Jon Hendricks was a walking thesaurus who could
write a lyric at the drop of a hat. British-born Annie Ross came from
a background in theatre and was the most accomplished singer of
the three.

Although the group was together for only four years, from the
end of 1957 till 1962, they never recorded a bad album. Their first,
Sing a Song of Basie (Verve), was a vocalese tribute to Count Basie
and is considered a classic. Its use of new recording technology
helped shatter the perception of what the human voice could do in
jazz. In all, Lambert, Hendricks & Ross recorded five albums. *The*

Hottest New Group in Jazz includes three albums recorded for Columbia – *The Hottest New Group in Jazz, Lambert, Hendricks & Ross Sing Ellington,* and *High Flying* – plus seven relatively unknown recordings.

Interestingly, most of these tracks were recorded in 1959 and 1960 (one of the most fruitful times for jazz), at the famed Columbia 30th Street recording studio in New York City, the same converted church used by Davis, Mingus, and Brubeck. Here, the best vocal jazz group of all time reinterpreted many of the best jazz compositions, such as Randy Weston's "Hi Fly," Dizzy Gillespie's "A Night in Tunisia," Horace Silver's "Home Cookin'," and Cannonball Adderley's "Sermonette."

The two-CD, thirty-nine-track package has numerous highlights. The brilliant "Charleston Alley" is their version of the Charlie Barnett instrumental that featured Peanuts Holland on trumpet on the original. Jon Hendricks wrote the lyrics for this version. Annie Ross sings the Peanuts trumpet solo and Dave Lambert performs Barnett's tenor sax solo.

"Moanin'" is a cool, sweet melody that was first written as an instrumental by Bobby Timmons when he was a member of Art Blakey's Jazz Messengers. Hendricks wrote his lyrics to the tune in just fifteen minutes. It is a classic.

"Twisted" is a blues and bebop standard written by tenor saxophonist Wardell Gray in 1949. Annie Ross wrote clever, comical lyrics that she delivered with tongue-twisting panache.

The tracks that comprised the concept album *Lambert, Hendricks & Ross Sing Ellington* are also included here. Astutely, for this record, the group blended familiar tunes with lesser-known ones. Among the better known are "Things Ain't What They Used to Be," "Caravan," and "Cottontail," which the trio interpret beautifully. "Cottontail" features Hendricks's lyrics about the Beatrix Potter characters Flopsie, Mopsie, and Peter Cottontail. Hendricks stepped forward on this album and wrote lyrics to the more obscure tunes "Happy Anatomy" and "Midnight Indigo" from Ellington's score to the Otto Preminger movie *Anatomy of a Murder*.

The selections on this retrospective confirm the genius of Jon Hendricks as both the principal lyricist and architect of the Lambert, Hendricks & Ross sound. Vocalese is a tough order to fill creatively, and Hendricks managed it by making the songs lyrically interesting, while retaining the integrity of the original music.

The interplay of their voices is a three-way musical conversation. Although the group's sound was sometimes flawed with imperfection, the magic lay in the sum of the three parts. Dave Lambert was weakest at singing, but his ability to arrange the voices was genius. Jon Hendricks had bad intonation and even sang slightly out of tune, but his enthusiasm and creativity propelled him forward. Annie Ross's voice was graced with incredible range. She could sing lyrics very quickly all the while enunciating clearly. Together, they revolutionized jazz singing.

■—————————————————————————————————————

Sony BMG #C2K 64933

CHARLES MINGUS, 1922–79
Mingus Ah Um
Recorded in New York City, May 1959

Charles Mingus is one of the music world's true characters and one of its most disturbing. A demanding, even bullying band-leader, a talented composer, and an innovative bassist, Mingus helped to free the bass from its traditional supportive role in jazz and make it an instrument that people listened to.

His unpredictable, volatile personality was cause for concern for many, and at one point Mingus spent time in New York's Bellevue psychiatric hospital. While working as a sideman in the early 1950s, he was the only musician Duke Ellington personally fired from his orchestra. When leading his own band, Mingus would sometimes stop playing mid-song to shush the audience or to berate a musician in his group for the inadequacy of his per-formance. During one concert, he punched trombonist Jimmy Knepper in the mouth.

Mingus Ah Um is the pinnacle of his career. It was recorded in the spring of 1959 and boasts the premiere of several exceptional songs. The best known is the melancholy ballad "Goodbye Pork Pie Hat." This is a salute to the great saxophonist Lester Young, who died seven weeks before this session. "Better Git It in Your Soul" was influenced by the church music Mingus listened to as a child in the Watts district of Los Angeles. It is a fabulous blues-gospel opus drenched with personality. The third acclaimed song that premiered on this disc is "Fables of Faubus." It was named after Orval Faubus, the Arkansas governor who in 1957 tried to block school integration in Little Rock, until President Eisenhower sent in the National Guard. Mingus had lyrics to go with the song but because of their topical nature Columbia refused to allow them to be recorded.

Mingus had a great ear for talent. For this album, he used John Handy and Booker Ervin on saxophones, Jimmy Knepper and Willie Dennis on trombones, Danny Richmond on drums, and Horace Parlan on piano. Collectively and individually their performances are yardsticks for musicians to measure themselves against.

Mingus Ah Um is an important jazz album to own. It is unique, unconventional, and brilliant.

■ ───────────────────────────────────────

Columbia/Legacy #CK 65512

DAVE BRUBECK, b. 1920
DAVE BRUBECK QUARTET
Time Out
Recorded in New York City, June–August 1959

Born to a Stockton, California, cattle-rancher who was also a rodeo champion, David Warren Brubeck was roping steers by the time he was fourteen and thinking of a career on the rodeo circuit. But his mother, a pianist and his first teacher, had a different dream for young Dave. It was undoubtedly her influence that encouraged his quantum leap from steer-wrestling to enrolment in classical music studies at the College of the Pacific in Stockton.

Brubeck went on to study theory with Darius Milhaud at Mills College in Oakland. While attending school, he played local clubs at night and met alto saxophonist Paul Desmond, an association that turned out to be one of the most successful in jazz history. They formed a quartet with bass and drums and soon became one of the most popular bands on the college concert circuit. They were also among the first to issue live recordings of their concerts, something that is commonplace today. The Dave Brubeck Quartet's recordings in the 1950s and 1960s were enormous commercial and artistic successes, propelling jazz onto the pop charts. "Take Five," a single release from the Quartet's 1959 album, *Time Out*, was the first jazz record to turn gold.

Time Out is a cool and melodic masterpiece, a glorious experiment in odd rhythms. In his liner notes to the 1997 reissue, Brubeck wrote, "The album defied all expert predictions, and instead of becoming an experimental dud, of interest only to other musicians, had caught on with the general public." *Time Out* was a potpourri of different time signatures that broke the 4/4 mould. They ranged from the awkward 5/4 of "Take Five" to the odd 9/8 of "Blue Rondo à la Turk," to the swinging 6/4 of "Pick Up Sticks" and "Everybody's Jumpin'."

The album's standout track, "Take Five," was written by saxophonist Paul Desmond. He said his inspiration for the song came from standing in front of a slot machine in Reno and trying to duplicate the rhythm, but in reality it was a blending of two themes that Brubeck suggested Desmond combine. The title was Brubeck's idea and met with resistance because Desmond didn't think that anyone would get the joke about the unusual metre. Desmond died in 1977 and willed his royalties from the song to the American Red Cross.

The brilliant "Blue Rondo à la Turk," with its classical overtones, comes from a rhythm Brubeck had heard being played by street musicians in Istanbul. The relaxing "Strange Meadow Lark" is derived from the call of a meadowlark, and "Kathy's Waltz" is named after his daughter. Every track is a keeper and is played with exuberance and virtuosity.

Brubeck's severest critics say he was heavy-handed and relied too much on playing block chords. This is a bit too harsh of a criticism, as his playing is often quite inspired. Brubeck's true genius, however, can be found in his compositions and in his selection of exceptional players.

Desmond's polished alto saxophone is the most recognizable part of the Dave Brubeck Quartet's sound. On *Time Out*, his interjected phrases are lyrical, playful, and melancholy. Joe Morello was a supremely accomplished drummer who was advanced rhythmically, and bassist Eugene Wright laid down a forceful, solid beat.

Time Out is an elegantly crafted record that keeps getting better with age.

■───────────────────────────────

Columbia/Legacy #CK 65122

GENE AMMONS, 1925–74
Greatest Hits, Vol. 1, The Sixties
Recorded in Englewood Cliffs, New Jersey, 1960–62

Gene Ammons is one of the unsung heros of the tenor sax. It is easy to understand why he's overlooked, because there is very little that is revolutionary or flowery about his work. Rather, he played the blues with a big, down-home, soulful sound. But he was plagued by a heroin addiction that prevented him from reaching his full potential.

Ammons grew up in Chicago, where his first musical role model was his father, the famous boogie-woogie pianist Albert Ammons. As a young man, Gene played in the bands of Billy Eckstine along with Charlie Parker, Miles Davis, and Dexter Gordon, and in Woody Herman's Thundering Herd, where he replaced Stan Getz. Ammons made his first record as a leader in 1947 and later collaborated with another prominent saxophonist, Sonny Stitt.

Ammons became addicted to heroin in the 1940s, and in 1958, he was charged with possession and sentenced to two years in jail. When he was released in 1960, he quickly made up for lost time by recording several albums. He was incarcerated again in 1962 for narcotics and released in 1969. Despite his time out of public view, he was a prolific recording artist, but as a result of his accelerated recording rate, he made some questionable choices in repertoire and production. Nevertheless, several of his recordings deserve to be among the top 101 for their juicy, soulful sound. In the years following his death, he became recognized as one of the stylists who helped to create "soul jazz," and in the 1990s a new, younger audience discovered his music as acid jazz grew in popularity.

A fine place to begin an Ammons collection is *The Greatest Hits, Vol. 1, The Sixties*. It highlights sessions Ammons recorded for the Prestige and Argo labels between June 16, 1960, and September 6, 1962, the short period between his two prison sentences. The sessions have excellent support from guitarists Kenny Burrell and Bucky Pizzarelli, Art Taylor on drums, pianists Hank Jones and Tommy Flanagan, Ray Barretto on congas, and organists Johnny "Hammond" Smith and Jack McDuff.

Despite the high level of musicianship from the various sidemen, these are Gene Ammons's songs, and his honey-toned sax is the focal point throughout. There is a beautiful acoustical symmetry between the tenor sax and organ on two selections, "Angel Eyes" and "Twisting the Jug," an Ammons original. He also wrote the groove-oriented "Seed Shack" and the percussive blues "Blue Ammons."

The standards include the Andy Williams hit "Canadian Sunset," "My Foolish Heart," "Angel Eyes," and "Exactly Like You." The album's standout track "Ca'Purange (Jungle Soul)" is from a 1962 session that placed Ammons firmly on the jazz charts. Unfortunately, the record was released to the public after he started serving time in late 1962. All of this material, and the standards in particular, had the potential to be lightweight if it hadn't been in the hands of a player such as Ammons. He had a big sound but he played with a startling intimacy and warmth that fascinated and seduced listeners.

All of this music sounds effortless, which is a remarkable achievement. As world-weary as Ammons's sound was, he knew how to squeeze every last note out of a song in his attempt to make music that reached the widest audience. What makes this album important is what Ammons excelled at doing, making music for people.

Gene Ammons had only two years of freedom in the 1960s, but musically they were a brilliant two years for him, and he left behind a great legacy.

■───

Prestige/Fantasy #OJCCD 6005-2

WAYNE SHORTER, b. 1933
The Classic Blue Note Recordings
Recorded in various locations between 1960 and 1989

As a tenor saxophonist, Wayne Shorter has few equals. As a composer, he is one of jazz's most innovative musicians. Shorter is the one player other players listen to when they want to have their backs scratched musically. Newcomers to jazz may well have heard Shorter playing and not known it. As a session musician, he's appeared on pop/rock recordings by Carlos Santana, the Rolling Stones, Joni Mitchell, and Steely Dan.

Shorter's career has been long and varied. After a very brief stint with Maynard Ferguson's big band, he was recruited by Art Blakey and his Jazz Messengers. Blakey served as an incubator for Shorter's musical ideas, and he soon became a prolific contributor to the band. However, it was as a member of the Miles Davis Quintet, also featuring Herbie Hancock, Tony Williams, and Ron Carter, that Shorter truly flourished. Davis's influence is apparent from the shift Shorter made as a player while with the quintet. His musical ideas became more focused and less reminiscent of John Coltrane, one of Shorter's early influences and the man he replaced in the quintet. Over the seven years he was in the group, Shorter made huge contributions to its overall sound.

After his tenure with Davis, Shorter, along with his friend, pianist Joe Zawinul, spent fifteen years leading one of the more innovative fusion groups in jazz, Weather Report. He also played as a sideman with other artists, but still found time to record under his own name. To date, his most creative and innovative work can be found on the double CD *The Classic Blue Note Recordings*. It features twenty-two selections Shorter recorded as both a leader and sideman over a twenty-nine-year period.

Disc one is the essential recording and features highlights from nine of his solo albums. These sessions include such sidemen as Lee Morgan, Freddie Hubbard, McCoy Tyner, Herbie Hancock, Ron Carter, Elvin Jones, Tony Williams, and John McLaughlin. Three of the songs are culled from Shorter's 1964 masterpiece *Speak No Evil*: "Witch Hunt," "Infant Eyes," and the title track, "Speak No Evil." All of them have become jazz standards but none surpasses Shorter's 1966 recording of "Footprints." It is the crown jewel and the composition that helped establish Shorter as a composer of note. He wrote it especially for Miles Davis and it appeared on his *Miles Smiles* album but Shorter's version predates it by eight months. This is classic Shorter, featuring exceptional writing and playing.

The second disc comprises ten Shorter compositions on which he was a featured sideman. Six of his most significant contributions from his years with Art Blakey and the Jazz Messengers (1959–64) are here, including the classics "The Chess Players" and the tribute to the great saxophonist Lester Young, "Lester Left Town." Also included are tunes he recorded with Freddie Hubbard, Lee Morgan, Michel Petrucciani, and The Manhattan Project, including versions of "Nefertiti" and "Limbo," songs from his days with Miles Davis.

Since the demise of Weather Report in 1985, Shorter has been in a creative slump that he can't seem to pull himself out of. Although *The Classic Blue Note Recordings* concentrates on the 1960s, it does serve as a reminder of Shorter's importance as one of jazz's leading figures over a long time. He is still a voice we should pay attention to in the hope he will return with another recording of merit.

■ —————————————————————————————

Blue Note #40856

■

OLIVER NELSON, 1932–75
Blues and the Abstract Truth
Recorded in Englewood Cliffs, New Jersey, February 1961

Oliver Nelson was a versatile arranger, composer, and saxophonist who is best known for composing the classic "Stolen Moments." He was a hobby model railroader who made the best of many of the opportunities presented to him. In 1951, he played with Louis Jordan's big band, followed by a stint in the Navy and four years studying music at university. He apprenticed in the bands of Erskine Hawkins, Louis Bellson, and later Quincy Jones.

The success of his landmark album *Blues and the Abstract Truth* gave him recognition, respect, and most importantly more work. It led to sessions with Cannonball Adderley, Jimmy Smith, Wes Montgomery, Buddy Rich, Nancy Wilson, and Stanley Turrentine. Outside of jazz it provided an opportunity to record with James Brown and the Temptations. His success attracted Hollywood's attention, and in 1967 he moved to Los Angeles. A Universal Studios executive had heard his work on a Jimmy Smith record and hired him.

In Los Angeles, Nelson wrote the music for many television shows, including *Columbo* with Peter Falk, *Ironside* starring Raymond Burr, and *Banachek* with George Peppard, and his best-known work, the theme for the *Six Million Dollar Man* with Lee Majors. In film, Nelson was equally as versatile and scored the *Last Tango in Paris* featuring the Argentinian sax player Gato Barbieri, and for the movie *Alfie*, he wrote lively arrangements as a musical backdrop for Sonny Rollins. Nelson died of a heart attack in 1975. He was forty-three.

Nelson's career-defining moment came in 1961 when record executive Creed Taylor signed him to a one-album deal for *Blues and the Abstract Truth*. The clever title for the release came from Taylor, who produced the session. Six songs were recorded in one day, on February 23, 1961, at Rudy Van Gelder's New Jersey studio. Nelson takes the blues and largely disregards its twelve-bar form, exploring the music in the post-bop style pioneered by Wayne Shorter and developed by Miles Davis and John Coltrane.

The lead track, "Stolen Moments," which Nelson wrote in 1960, is one of the most important jazz songs ever. Nelson made the best use of the musical talents booked to play on the date with an emotional trumpet solo by Freddie Hubbard, followed by Eric Dolphy on flute, then Nelson on sax, and lastly Bill Evans on piano. The track consists of three melodic ideas that through magic become one. It is a musical masterpiece.

The next best known, and perhaps the most unusual composition on the disc, is the rousing "Hoe-Down." Nelson borrows heavily from the American composer Aaron Copland on this. Once again, Hubbard is on trumpet, but Dolphy moves to sax, and Roy Haynes is on drums.

The bopish "Cascades" started as a saxophone exercise Nelson composed in college. It is a beautiful vehicle for Nelson, Hubbard, and Evans to solo. Evans, in particular, makes a strong statement as his solo builds in intensity. "Teenie's Blues" is a blues dedicated to Nelson's young sister and features Dolphy and Nelson playing the melodic line on alto saxophones.

Blues and the Abstract Truth is a giant recording in the history of jazz.

■ ──

Impulse! #IMPD154

DAVE BRUBECK QUARTET
Time Further Out
Recorded in New York City, May 3–June 8, 1961

In the 1950s, Dave Brubeck's collaboration with Paul Desmond made the Dave Brubeck Quartet one of the most popular bands in jazz and helped fuel the genre's revival. After the success of their seminal and wildly popular *Time Out* album, dozens of other jazz musicians were inspired to try non-traditional time signatures, and the quartet itself continued to experiment, releasing several more albums, including *Time Further Out, Time in Outer Space*, and *Time Changes*.

Time Further Out, originally released in 1961, is just as spectacular as the earlier album and deserves to be just as well known. Once again, Brubeck on piano, Desmond on sax, Joe Morello on drums, and Eugene Wright on bass bring their innovative rhythms, signatures, and odd metres to bear, this time on a collection of compositions based on twelve-bar blues. The album is intended as a jazz interpretation of Spanish painter Joan Miró's 1925 painting *Miró Reflections*, which is featured on the album cover. In the original liner notes, Brubeck wrote, "For those who like to ponder such topics, many a long winter evening can be devoted to discussing the relationship between painting and music. Suffice it to say that it was just such reflections, on the specific relationships of Miró, painting, and jazz which brought about the music of this album."

In August 1996, Dave Brubeck shared some new observations on the re-release of *Time Further Out*, which includes bonus tracks discovered when the tapes from the original recording session were played. "Perhaps Desmond and I were just trying to relax

before confronting the challenges of new odd-metered material,"
he said. "When I reviewed the original liner notes I wrote 35 years
ago, I had to smile at my self-conscious effort to explain the sig-
nificance of the various time signatures. Nowadays, excursions
into 9/8, 7/4, or 5/4 are commonplace."

"Unsquare Dance," inspired by African drumming rhythms,
netted the quartet another hit single, and its B-side, "It's a Raggy
Waltz," delivers a syncopated quality that gives an old-time rag
complex rhythmic variations. "Bluette" is a pianistic waltz in 3/4
time, often described as the blues played by Frédéric Chopin, and
"Far More Blue" features a solo excursion by Brubeck in the 5/4
time signature that Desmond and Morello originally explored in
"Take Five." "Far More Drums" showcases Morello and Desmond,
both of them clearly comfortable in 5/4 time, while "Maori Blues"
is in a 6/4 time that Brubeck first heard while visiting New Zealand.

■ ───

Sony BMG #64668

■

BILL EVANS, 1929–80
Bill Evans Trio: Sunday at the Village Vanguard
Recorded in New York City, June 25, 1961

Bill Evans is the most significant jazz pianist of the last forty years. He influenced a wide range of players, including Chick Corea, Keith Jarrett, and Herbie Hancock. Evans was a brilliant player who created some of the most complex, calming music in jazz, but offstage, he was an enormously troubled individual. An introvert, he seemed unready for the spotlight and spent most of his adult life addicted to drugs. In the fall of 1979, I visited him in his New Jersey apartment and was struck by the condition of his hands. The tools he used to deliver his craft were swollen and scarred from injecting drugs. It was the ultimate act of self-destruction for a pianist. He died the following year.

Evans's musical brilliance came largely from two areas, pop and classical music. For him, melody was paramount. He relied heavily on American popular song for a portion of his repertoire and his selections were flawless. The introspective nature of his playing was very appealing and owed a large debt to the French classical composers Debussy and Ravel.

Bill Evans Trio: Sunday at the Village Vanguard started as just another gig in a jazz club in New York City, but the subsequent recording by one of the greatest trios in jazz – Evans on piano, Scott LaFaro on bass, and Paul Motian on drums – is a masterpiece.

The Village Vanguard, a basement jazz club on 7th Avenue in New York's Greenwich Village, still exists. On a summer Sunday afternoon on June 25, 1961, the trio descended a long flight of stairs into the damp, dimly lit club. Their matinee performance consisted of five sets spread over two-and-a-half hours. Live recordings were still relatively new to the world of jazz, and the portable recording gear was visible to everyone who used the washroom that afternoon.

Thirteen songs were performed, several more than once. They were intimate interpretations of standards, including "My Man's Gone Now" and "All of You," and compositions by bassist LaFaro, including "Jade Visions" and "Gloria's Step." Six songs made it to the original edition of this album, but the CD version includes five bonus tracks that are repeats.

Bill Evans Trio: Sunday at the Village Vanguard is a recording that changed how trios were perceived in jazz. Before it, the trio was often just a vehicle for the pianist to solo, with the other musicians relegated to the role of accompanists. In the hands of Bill Evans, Scott LaFaro, and Paul Motian, the trio became a whole, with each instrument playing a prominent role. The interplay and connectedness between the three was astonishing. It is worth noting that just days after this recording took place, LaFaro was killed in a car accident. It took Evans some time to recover from his loss.

■
_____

Riverside #RCD 9376

■

CANNONBALL ADDERLEY, 1928–75
The Best of Cannonball Adderley, The Capitol Years
Recorded in Belgium, San Francisco, New York, and
Los Angeles, 1962–69

Cannonball Adderley was an affable, good-natured guy, and a great, folksy communicator. The blues-based tone he found on his alto saxophone was distinctive and helped to define the hard bop sound, a more intense, more melodic evolution from bebop. He was liked and respected by other musicians; he even played on Miles Davis's influential *Kind of Blue* album. Later Adderley managed to cross over to the pop charts with a hit.

He was also an insatiable music fan and a talent scout who would give struggling musicians a break either by hiring them for his group or producing their records, sometimes both. Adderley was the one who brought Wes Montgomery to the attention of Orrin Keepnews at Riverside Records, and he produced the debut recording by Chuck Mangione.

Born in Florida, Julian "Cannonball" Adderley started his career as a high-school band director in Fort Lauderdale, where he was a local celebrity. His nickname was a variation on Cannibal, a name given to him in his youth because of his appetite. In 1955, during a visit to New York City to look into continuing his music studies, he sat in one night with Oscar Pettiford at the Café Bohemia. He grabbed everyone's attention and was hailed as a potential star and most likely to be the next Charlie Parker, who had recently died. It was enough to persuade Adderley (and his brother, Nat, who played cornet) to move to New York and sign with Mercury Records. After an unsuccessful try at leading his own band, Adderley joined the Miles Davis Quintet, and stayed with Davis for four years. In 1959, he and Nat formed their own, very successful quintet, signing with the Riverside label and later Capitol Records, where he recorded close to twenty albums. There was a shift in Adderley's sound through the years, and the recordings he made for Capitol have a highly appealing, gritty down-home sound based on gospel and blues.

It is difficult to recommend just one album by Adderley, as so much of what he recorded is worth hearing. But a good place to start is *The Best of Cannonball Adderley, The Capitol Years.* One of Adderley's strengths was his ability to recognize imaginative young talent, and he found it in Josef Zawinul, the young Austrian he hired to play piano. Zawinul turned out to be a prolific composer and often inspired pianist.

This album features one studio and seven live tracks recorded between 1962 and 1969. Zawinul's "Mercy, Mercy, Mercy" (which went to number ten on the pop charts), "Country Preacher" (written about Rev. Jesse Jackson), and "Walk Tall" are all soulful classics. Two of the songs here were recorded for the Riverside label, with flautist and tenor sax player Yusef Lateef – "Work Song" (written by Nat Adderley) and "Jive Samba." Don't let the budget appearance of this package deceive you; the contents are swingin'.

Capitol/EMI #95482

HERBIE HANCOCK, b. 1940
The Essential Herbie Hancock
Recorded in Englewood Cliffs, New Jersey; New York; and San Francisco, 1962–95

Herbie Hancock is one of the most commercially and artistically successful artists in jazz, and many of his compositions have become standards. He created a style all his own that was harmonically advanced for his time, and his crystalline playing and virtuosic soloing have made him one of the most influential pianists since Bill Evans. Hancock could have been content with this and concentrated on playing acoustic improvisation, but much like his mentor and employer, Miles Davis, he ignored musical boundaries and crossed over into pop, rock, rhythm and blues, and funk. And to all these genres, he brought his distinctive musical voice.

Hancock is a classically trained child prodigy, who performed a Mozart piano concerto with the Chicago Symphony Orchestra at the age of eleven. He started playing jazz in high school, influenced by the music of Bill Evans and Oscar Peterson. Hancock thought he would never be able to make a living as a musician, so for his first year at university he studied electrical engineering. But his heart wasn't in it, and in his second year he shifted his major to music.

There is no shortage of exceptional recordings by Hancock to add to your collection. The difficult task is choosing the right one. For a sampling of the broadest spectrum of music I've selected *The Essential Herbie Hancock*. It is a two-disc compilation covering Hancock's recordings for seven labels over a forty-year career.

Many of his most important compositions are included; there's a sampling of solo work, as well as previously neglected tracks and a few others that are curiosities.

The funky "Chameleon" is from Hancock's 1974 *Headhunters* album, which is one of the best-selling records in the history of jazz. Hancock had been listening to Sly and the Family Stone and used many of the rhythms he heard in their music. The opening riff was borrowed from Sly's masterpiece "Thank You for Letting Me Be Myself." It is a delicious combination of jazz and rock and a churning blend of woodwinds, percussion, and keyboards.

"Watermelon Man" was inspired by the horse-drawn delivery carts that Hancock remembers hearing rattle along the cobblestone alleys of his hometown, Chicago. He wanted to duplicate the rhythm he heard in the voices of the drivers as they sold their melons. The song was the standout track on Hancock's debut album *Taking Off* and features Freddie Hubbard on trumpet and Dexter Gordon on sax. "Watermelon Man" was a hit for Mongo Santamaria in 1963 and then again in 1974 for Hancock's group, the Headhunters.

The delicately melodic "Tell Me a Bedtime Story" is a song Hancock recorded for his daughter in 1969. The instrumentation on this one is an appealing and unusual combination of sax, flute, tuba, and electric piano. It is one of the reasons, decades after its release, that the song still sounds interesting.

From 1965 there is the title song from the album *Maiden Voyage*, a song that has become a standard in jazz. Tuneful and musically haunting, it started out as a jingle for Yardley's Men's Cologne. This session featured the Miles Davis rhythm section of Ron Carter on bass and Tony Williams on drums, with help from trumpet player Freddie Hubbard and saxophonist George Coleman.

The Essential Herbie Hancock also provides a look at other aspects of Hancock's personality. "Circles" is from the five-year period he was a member of Miles Davis's group. The players – Miles on trumpet, Tony Williams on drums, Ron Carter on bass,

Wayne Shorter on sax, and Hancock on piano – play as one, and
this recording raised the musical bar a notch or two higher. Also
included is a session with saxophonist Sonny Rollins playing the
classic "'Round Midnight."

Altogether there are twenty songs. There's one from Hancock's
days in the trio, another from his Davis tribute band, VSOP, and
several of his rather nondescript jazz fusion songs. By today's standards, some of these sound dated and seem like musical curiosities.
In complete contrast, the acoustic music from the 1960s still sounds
amazing. This is a great double CD to have in your collection, but
had it been reduced to a single album, it would be perfect.

■

Columbia/Legacy #94593

SHEILA JORDAN, b. 1928
Portrait of Sheila
Recorded in Englewood Cliffs, New Jersey,
September and October 1962

Sheila Jordan provides one of life's musical pleasures. She is a warm, funny, and self-deprecating person, and a perpetually innovative singer. She is an "underground" vocalist, who is equally at home singing avant-garde projects or straight-ahead jazz. Her importance in jazz is not reflected by her CD sales, but by her influence on other singers.

She was born Sheila Jeannette Dawson to a teenage mother in Detroit and raised by her grandparents in a coal-mining town in Pennsylvania where alcoholism and poverty was all around her. She started singing to herself at the age of three, and as a teenager she sang in Detroit clubs. Then in 1950, she moved to New York City to be close to Charlie Parker and the burgeoning bebop scene. There she married Parker's pianist, Duke Jordan, and studied music with Charles Mingus and Lennie Tristano. Along the way there was a struggle with drugs and alcohol, and it wasn't until 1962 that she made her first album, *Portrait of Sheila*.

Jordan was uncompromising in the musical statement she intended to make and it was twelve years before she recorded *Confirmation*, her second album, in 1974. She spent a good portion of the 1960s and 1970s working as an administrative assistant in an ad agency and performing in the evenings, on weekends, and holidays.

In 2004, Jordan received the prestigious Lil Hardin Armstrong Jazz Heritage Award at the International Association for Jazz

Educators conference in New York City. There she sat with a number of other singers on a panel called "Singing for Our Supper: Vocalists in the Jazz Marketplace." Sheila remarked ruefully, "For most of my life I've been singing for snacks."

For an artist in her seventies, Jordan is decidedly under-recorded. Her delightful *Portrait of Sheila* is her best album, and recording it was a bold move for Blue Note because they recorded only instrumentalists. It does reflect the short length of vinyl albums made at the time, clocking in at under forty minutes. But for all it is short, it is powerful. It is obvious from the first track that Jordan is one of a small group of jazz singers who is entirely original. Her musical trademark is her repeated changes of pitch, which can confuse a first-time listener.

The sound is musically sparse, with Jordan backed by just a trio. Barry Galbraith is on guitar; Denzil Best plays drums, and the peerless Steve Swallow is on bass. On one of the album's standout tracks, "Dat Dere," she sings with only Swallow's bass, and on "Who Can I Turn To?" there is simply Galbraith's guitar. On "Hum Drum Blues" and "Baltimore Oriole" she is accompanied by just bass and drums. On the latter, there is an exquisite passage where Steve Swallow plays in harmony with Jordan. This skeletal sound works to Jordan's advantage; there is no musical confusion. It sounds as if she is focused on listening to what the others are playing, particularly when only one musician is accompanying her. This is jazz without a safety net.

■ ───

Blue Note #89002

OSCAR PETERSON, b. 1925
Night Train
Recorded in New York City, December 1962

Although already known in Canada, the name Oscar Peterson wasn't widely recognized elsewhere until Norman Granz presented him to the rest of the world in a Jazz at the Philharmonic concert at Carnegie Hall in 1949. That dazzling performance launched his stunning soar to the top, where he has remained unchallenged ever since.

In Gene Lee's book *Jazz Lives*, Hank Jones (who Peterson says was *his* teacher) said, "Oscar Peterson is head-and-shoulders above any pianist alive today. Oscar is at the apex. He is the crowning ruler of all the pianists in the jazz world." Few would question that statement.

Peterson has played solo recitals all over the world, worked with the biggest of the big bands, mastered gospel, European classical music, and, always, the blues. But from the time he started leading trios in the early 1950s, it is the trio that is regarded by many – including O.P. himself – as the best, certainly his favourite, setting for his unlimited gifts.

That has never been more clearly articulated than in this re-release of the famous *Night Train* album featuring the Oscar Peterson Trio. It is not just one of the talented trios that he has continued to lead on stages all over the world for decades. This is *the* Oscar Peterson Trio – O.P., Ray Brown, and Ed Thigpen – the combination of artists that shows musical communication at its most sensitive. It's been said that Ray Brown is to the bass what Oscar Peterson is to the piano. The bass solo he delivers in the trio's treatment of Duke Ellington's "Night Train" leaves no doubt about that. And Ed Thigpen, "the thinking man's drummer," lays down a tight rhythmic carpet throughout.

The re-release of *Night Train* includes six tunes that didn't make it to the album when it was first recorded in 1962, including a lovely treatment of two unlikely jazz tunes, Cole Porter's "My Heart Belongs to Daddy," and "Volare," notable here for the Ahmad Jamal–type chord voicings Peterson brings to it. The seventeen tracks are mostly jazz standards, but the music ranges from lively swing numbers to breathtakingly beautiful ballads. The one original song is Peterson's own "Hymn to Freedom."

The album notes promise that "no material here requires musicological analysis: the music speaks for itself." And indeed it does. The tunes range from Ellington's classic "C-Jam Blues," where the trio abides by Ellington's 1942 arrangement, and Milt Jackson's "Bags' Groove" blues anthem, which Peterson plays in the key of G rather than the customary F, to "Hymn to Freedom," which closes out the CD with gospel-like grace.

■————————————————————————————

Verve #3145214402

KENNY BURRELL, b. 1931
Midnight Blue
Recorded in Englewood Cliffs, New Jersey, January 7, 1963

Kenny Burrell is a highly respected jazz artist and educator. He is a favourite of musicians around the world and was Duke Ellington's choice guitarist. That's high praise indeed. Over the years he has played with many of jazz's best: Oscar Peterson, Coleman Hawkins, Billie Holiday, Benny Goodman, Sonny Rollins, and John Coltrane. He is a prolific artist who has recorded almost one hundred albums and has appeared as a sideman on more than two hundred. As a jazz educator, Burrell developed in 1978 the first regular college course on the music of Ellington taught in the United States. Today he is a professor and the director of the Jazz Studies Program at UCLA.

Burrell was born in Detroit and grew up at a very fertile time when Thad Jones, Barry Harris, Tommy Flanagan, Yuseff Lateef, Frank Foster, Paul Chambers, and Donald Byrd were all up-and-coming jazz musicians. He started playing the guitar at age twelve, and at nineteen, he had his first taste of a recording studio when he appeared as sideman on a Dizzy Gillespie session. His musical influences included two important guitarists in jazz: Charlie Christian, the inventor of modern jazz guitar, and Oscar Moore, who was Nat King Cole's guitarist.

The genesis for his most popular album, *Midnight Blue*, came during a conversation Burrell had with Blue Note owner Alfred Lion about doing an album based on the blues. Burrell was so focused on the album and the statement he wanted to make that he even came up with the concept for the album cover.

Burrell thought carefully about the sound he wanted on the album and spent some time looking for the right combination to work with percussionist Ray Barretto. Stanley Turrentine's soulfulness as a sax player and his ability to play the blues made him a natural choice. The other band members were Bill English on drums, Ray Barretto on conga, and Major Holley Jr. on bass. Burrell decided there would be no piano on this session. He felt the sound wasn't required for the blues he wanted to produce.

The session took place on one day on April 21, 1967, and featured one standard song and seven Burrell originals. The album was highlighted by several tracks. "Chitlins Con Carne" has a touch of the bossa nova but at its core it is a blues number, featuring Stanley Turrentine's creamy playing. "Midnight Blue" is one of the few tracks not featuring Turrentine, but Burrell takes care of it all, laying down a firm beat and never over-playing.

"Soul Lament" features Burrell playing solo electric guitar. Its overtones of Charlie Christian's style and of flamenco are a strong reminder of just how much music Burrell has listened to.

"Gee Baby Ain't I Good to You" is the only standard song on the album. It dates back to McKinney's Cotton Pickers in the 1930s and was later a hit for Nat King Cole. That version featured one of Burrell's guitar influences, Oscar Moore.

Midnight Blue is a warm, intimate, and relaxed recording that's perfect for listening to at midnight. Kenny Burrell is a lyrical, soulful musician who does not waste notes, and the band is superb. *Midnight Blue* is one album I can guarantee you will listen to again and again.

■ ───

Blue Note #95335

JOHNNY HARTMAN, 1923–83
John Coltrane and Johnny Hartman
Recorded in Englewood Cliffs, New Jersey, March 7, 1963

Singer Johnny Hartman's lack of popularity is one of the jazz world's injustices. Hartman was one of the very best romantic balladeers. His warm baritone voice combined with his spacious lyrical interpretation of a song was intoxicating. But for most of his performing and recording years, he was a cult figure who struggled for recognition, and he didn't become well known until twelve years after his death. That's when Clint Eastwood selected some of his songs to be used in the movie *The Bridges of Madison County*.

Hartman was born in Chicago and grew up singing in a church choir and the glee club in high school. He received a scholarship to study voice at the Chicago Musical College, then served in the American forces during the Second World War. After leaving the army, Hartman won a singing contest organized by pianist and bandleader Earl "Fatha" Hines. He sang and toured with Hines for a while and then worked with Dizzy Gillespie's big band. A two-month gig with Erroll Garner's trio followed before Hartman struck out on his own.

Of all the recordings released while Hartman was alive, his most successful was *John Coltrane and Johnny Hartman*. Its genesis came from the night Hartman sat in with Coltrane's quartet at Birdland in New York City. A few weeks later they were in the studio recording.

Because of Coltrane's stature in jazz, it is often thought that this is simply an album "with" Hartman, but there is no doubt it is equally his and Coltrane's album from start to finish. The album itself gives the evidence in the near-perfect blending of Coltrane's soothing tenor sax and Hartman's elegant voice.

John Coltrane and Johnny Hartman is a work of art that should be in every collection. There are six ballad standards here, including "They Say It's Wonderful," "Dedicated to You," "My One and Only Love," "Lush Life," "You Are Too Beautiful," and "Autumn Serenade." Hartman sings with such a good rhythmic feel and always knows where the groove is. He doesn't depart from the melody yet somehow manages to personalize each one of the songs.

Coltrane's performance is one of his most lyrical, and you can hear that he is thinking about the lyrics as he is playing. There are times you hardly notice the change from horn to voice. Remember that this was a period when Coltrane was very serious about his art and was being heralded for being on the cutting edge. Hartman was more cheerful about his endeavours, but certainly no less committed to his work. It is the only time Coltrane recorded with a singer; perhaps he viewed this session as a way to help a talent who deserved wider recognition.

The one-day recording session took place on March 7, 1963, at Rudy Van Gelder's famed studio in Englewood Cliffs, New Jersey, and Coltrane later did overdubs and added obbligato sax phrases behind Hartman's vocals on "My One and Only Love," "Lush Life," and "You Are Too Beautiful."

This unlikely pairing of Coltrane and Hartman was well received by the public. Hartman tried to recapture the feeling on other sessions without Coltrane later in the 1960s, but the music scene was changing. The British musical invasion had started, and the appeal of American popular song was on the decline.

■ ─────────────────────────────────────

Impulse! #GRD157

STAN GETZ, 1927–91
Getz/Gilberto with Antonio Carlos Jobim
Recorded in New York City, March 18 and 19, 1963

Stan Getz coaxed the most sorrowful, sentimental sounds from his tenor saxophone. As jazz critic Whitney Balliett once said, he had "a lovely tone, the kind of tone one would want to go home to."

No doubt about it, Getz was a troubled individual. At seventeen, he was already an alcoholic and, not long afterward, became addicted to heroin. He did not stop using until he was sixty and attempted suicide several times over the course of his life. His mood fluctuation was cause for concern for many and was the impetus for Zoot Sims's description of his friend: "Yeah, Stan's a nice bunch of guys."

Getz started playing professionally in New York City when he was fifteen. Just one year later, he was playing with grown men in Jack Teagarden's group. He then had steady employment in the big bands of Stan Kenton, Jimmy Dorsey, and Benny Goodman. It was while he was with Woody Herman that he and the other saxophonists in the band, Serge Chaloff, Zoot Sims, and Al Cohn, were nicknamed the Four Brothers. Getz's resplendent sound made him the most popular of the four, and he soon struck out on his own.

Getz's supreme accomplishment is the masterpiece *Getz/ Gilberto with Antonio Carlos Jobim*. Originally released in March 1964, this partnership between Getz and guitarist João Gilberto is one of the few jazz albums to reach number one on the pop charts. It spent almost two years there and won four Grammy Awards. Several of the songs, including "Desafinado," "Corcovado," and "Girl from

Ipanema," have become jazz standards. Their familiarity inspires both love and hatred amongst jazz fans.

Getz/Gilberto is one of those rare albums of musical magic that is bewildering to listen to. Several elements combine to bewitch the listener: Getz's genius for playing the shapely, imaginative melodies composed by the father of the bossa nova, Antonio Carlos Jobim (who also played piano on the session); João Gilberto's exotic guitar playing and his bittersweet Portuguese vocals; and Gilberto's wife Astrud's detached, icy reading of "The Girl from Ipanema" and "Corcovado," which still seduces. Astrud's singing is made even more charming because her presence on the hit record was a fluke. Stan asked her to sing at a rehearsal because she was the only Brazilian he knew who could speak English. Her performance was so sensual Getz asked her, over protests from Antonio and João that she wasn't a professional singer, to sing on the album. It was a smart move because her English interpretation of the Portuguese lyrics helped make the songs accessible for a North American audience.

■ ──────────────────────────────────────

Verve #3145214142

LEE MORGAN, 1938–72
The Sidewinder
Recorded in Englewood Cliffs, New Jersey, December 1963

Lee Morgan was a child prodigy. At age fifteen he was already leading his own group in Philadelphia, having picked up the trumpet for the first time one year earlier. Esteemed trumpeter Dizzy Gillespie recruited him to play in his big band when he was just seventeen. There he assumed the trumpet solo duties on Gillespie's signature piece, "A Night in Tunisia." During the two years he was with Gillespie, he also recorded his first album for Blue Note. When he was nineteen, he played impressive solos on two landmark albums, John Coltrane's *Blue Train* and Jimmy Smith's *The Sermon*.

Morgan was twenty when he joined Art Blakey's Jazz Messengers, making a strong contribution to their sound, particularly on the soulful, bluesy tunes in the Blakey book. Over the course of his career, he was one of the most prolific Blue Note artists, and recorded twenty-five albums for the label.

He was dependent on heroin for much of his adult life. In 1960, Morgan left the Jazz Messengers, withdrew from music, and went home to Philadelphia to kick the habit. Upon returning, he heard a musical tribute on the radio that said he was dead, which gave him pause.

In 1963, Morgan recorded his Blue Note comeback album *The Sidewinder*. The title song was a funky, soulful, blues-based dance number that was inspired by the bad-guy roles he saw on television. It was edited down to a 45-rpm single that proved so popular, it pushed the album into the top twenty-five of the pop album charts. Later, Chrysler used it for a television commercial during the 1965 World Series. The sales from the album helped save Blue Note from potential bankruptcy.

The Sidewinder is a very satisfying album. Morgan, who composed all five songs, was a good, muscular, no-frills trumpet player and an ace technician. "Totem Pole" was named for the effect of Morgan's alternation with saxophonist Joe Henderson on a group of six notes they play going into and coming out of the song. "Gary's Notebook" is a blues that was named after a friend of Morgan's who, no matter what he was doing, always carried a notebook in case he had to write down an idea. "Hocus Pocus" and "Boy, What a Night" are both freewheeling, blues-based blowing sessions.

The musicians are of particular note: Joe Henderson on tenor saxophone, Barry Harris on piano, Bob Cranshaw on bass, and Billy Higgins on drums. It is a no-frills band that swings hard and plays with bite and attitude.

Morgan's life ended tragically when, on February 19, 1972, Helen More, his common-law wife, shot and killed him during an argument at Slugs, a jazz club on Manhattan's Lower East Side. Morgan was thirty-three years old.

■

Blue Note #95332

ANTONIO CARLOS BRASILEIRO DE ALMEIDA
JOBIM, 1927–94
The Man from Ipanema
Recorded in Rio de Janeiro, Los Angeles, New York, and Englewood
Cliffs, New Jersey, 1963–94

Antonio Carlos Jobim is one of the most outstanding composers
of the twentieth century. Many of Jobim's beautiful compositions,
including "The Girl from Ipanema," "One Note Samba,"
"Corcovado," "How Insensitive," and "Waters of March," have
become standards around the world. He ranks with such other
composers as Cole Porter, John Lennon and Paul McCartney,
George Gershwin, Hoagy Carmichael, and Paul Simon.

At the end of the 1950s, Jobim, along with lyricist Vinicius de
Moraes and guitarist João Gilberto, played a role in creating
Brazil's distinctive bossa nova music. Jobim had been influenced
by the West Coast cool-jazz sound of Gerry Mulligan and Chet
Baker and the harmonies of the French Impressionist composers
Debussy and Ravel. But his musical roots lay in Brazil's fast and
energetic samba and the laid-back ballads of the Portuguese set-
tlers. Jobim's composing style began to take focus when he
combined these elements and helped to create a fresh sound, bossa
nova. He had his first big hit in 1962 when Stan Getz and Charlie
Byrd recorded "Desafinado."

Then one song changed Jobim's life forever. A tall and tan
and young and lovely sixteen-year-old girl, Heloisa Pinheiro,
went for her early morning walk on Ipanema Beach one day in
the summer of 1962. Jobim and de Moraes observed her from

their second-floor table at the Veloso Bar, where they could sometimes be found consoling themselves after escapades the night before. The classic "The Girl from Ipanema" was born.

It is essential to have music by Jobim in your collection. There are a number of single-CD compilations that are excellent, but my recommendation is a three-CD set called *The Man from Ipanema*. The fifty-five songs in this collection showcase the many aspects of Jobim: as a pianist, guitarist, vocalist, and, most importantly, composer. The three CDs cover Jobim's complete association with Verve and its associated labels from his first recording date to his last.

The first CD is comprised of vocal versions of Jobim's work. There are the obvious selections, with Jobim playing and singing in Portuguese and English on "Jazz Samba," "Waters of March," and "Dindi." His near-whisper singing sounds slightly amateurish, but it is the charm and sensuality of his voice and the absolute genius of his compositions that redeem him. The set also digs deep and features three selections in Portuguese from the classic 1974 recording Jobim made with singer Elis Regina. There is also Jobim's rendition of the comical, self-mocking "Chansong." This is music in the spirit of Debussy, Ravel, and Villa Lobos.

The second CD features instrumental recordings, including selections from Jobim's first North American release, *The Composer of "Desafinado" Plays*. These 1963 sessions feature the exquisite arrangements of Claus Ogerman.

The third CD has, side by side, various versions of his classic songs played by a number of artists, including Luyiz Bonfa, Stan Getz, and Charlie Byrd. The most cherished recordings are the three that were performed on April 9, 1994, at Verve Records' fiftieth-anniversary bash at Carnegie Hall in New York City. "The Girl from Ipanema," "Desafinado," and "How Insensitive," featuring Jobim in three settings: with a quartet featuring Joe Henderson and Charlie Haden; in a duo with Pat Metheny; and then solo as he sings and plays the piano. This was the last public performance Jobim gave before he died in December 1994.

■ ──

Verve #314525880z

JOHN LESLIE "WES" MONTGOMERY, 1925–68
Wes Montgomery's Finest Hour
Recorded in Englewood Cliffs, New Jersey, and New York, 1964–68

For many fans, Wes Montgomery is to jazz what Jimi Hendrix is to rock or what B.B. King is to the blues.

After listening to an album by jazz guitarist Charlie Christian (who died aged twenty-five in 1942), Montgomery went out the next day and bought a guitar and amp. At the age of eighteen he taught himself to play the guitar. In an attempt to subdue the sound of his guitar and not wake the neighbours when he was practising, Wes didn't use a pick and instead used his thumb to pluck and brush the strings. This unusual approach not only muted his playing, it produced the warm, rich, expressive sound he became famous for.

In 1948, Montgomery received his first break when he joined vibraphonist Lionel Hampton's orchestra. Montgomery's fear of flying meant he drove from gig to gig, and his small salary made it difficult to support his family. After two years he returned to Indianapolis, where his life became even more exhausting. He worked as a welder from 7:00 a.m. to 3:00 p.m. After work he'd grab a few hours of sleep, and then from 9:00 p.m. until 2:00 a.m. he played at the Turf Bar, and from 2:30 a.m. until 5:00 a.m. another gig at the Missile Room, an after-hours club. It was at the Missile Room that Montgomery was heard by saxophonist Cannonball Adderley. The next day, Adderley contacted his friend and record producer Orrin Keepnews and persuaded him to check out Montgomery. Within hours Keepnews was following Montgomery from gig to gig in Indianapolis, and by the next dawn had signed him to Riverside. Two weeks later he made his first record for the label.

Montgomery's recording career can be divided in two. The recordings he made for Riverside, from 1959 to 1963, were straight-ahead jazz albums that were critically well received but achieved limited commercial success. When Riverside declared bankruptcy in 1963, Montgomery signed with Verve and later A&M and embarked on the second and most commercially satisfying segment of his career. He recorded several exceptional albums for both labels, most notably *The Incredible Jazz Guitar* for Riverside and *Smokin' at the Half Note* for Verve. Interestingly, Pat Metheny says the latter is the greatest guitar album ever made.

Wes Montgomery's Finest Hour is essential listening and consists of sixteen selections he recorded from 1964 to 1968 for Verve and A&M. Montgomery's producer on these sessions is the often maligned Creed Taylor. He encouraged Montgomery to play in a more popular style by selecting covers of many of the pop tunes of the day and using arrangements that favoured seductive strings, bouncy horns, and Latin percussion. These are the sessions that made Montgomery financially secure and provided him with his two Grammy Awards.

"Goin' Out of My Head," a hit for Little Anthony and the Imperials, is one of the highlights and the song that made him a star. It runs just over two minutes and is magnificently executed. Montgomery's solo is melodic and hard driving. Johnny Mandel's beautiful "The Shadow of Your Smile" is played with just the right amount of delicate improvisation. Antonio Carlos Jobim's "Once I Loved" is unhurried and breezy. "Impressions," with Jimmy Cobb on drums, Wynton Kelly on piano, and Paul Chambers on bass, is from Montgomery's landmark *Smokin' at the Half Note*, and features Montgomery raw, with none of the arrangements that some people find annoying. Also included are many of Montgomery's compositions, such as "Twisted Blues," "Bumpin' on Sunset," and "Road Song."

There are unbeatable rhythm sections featured on many of the sessions, including Herbie Hancock, Roger Kellaway, and Wynton Kelly on piano; Ron Carter, Bob Cranshaw, and Paul Champers on bass; and Grady Tate and Jimmy Cobb on drums. As a soloist, Montgomery is articulate and seldom struggles with the arrangements, which were written by three of the best: Claus Ogerman, Don Sebesky, and Oliver Nelson. Montgomery was a natural musician, but he could not read music and was often uncomfortable around "schooled" musicians, so the arrangements were recorded after the principal sessions took place.

The commercial nature of these recordings inspires both love and hatred in the jazz community, but few can deny the tonal beauty and suave phrasing of Montgomery's playing. If you are new to his music or jazz guitar albums, there is no better place to start than *Wes Montgomery's Finest Hour*.

Five weeks after he played "Road Song," at the age of forty-five, Montgomery died from a heart attack. He left behind his wife, Serene, and seven children. His grandson, actor Anthony Montgomery, who starred in *Star Trek Enterprise*, is preparing a documentary on Wes Montgomery's life.

■ _____

Verve #0694906682

OSCAR PETERSON, b. 1925
The Canadiana Suite
Recorded in New York City, September 9, 1964

Home is an idea that most of us are familiar with. I call it an idea because that's what it is – something intangible, a place we hold in our hearts and our minds. Home defines us, finds us, gives us refuge, solace, and comfort. Home can be made of bricks and mortar, a house or a town or a city. It can even be a person. But whatever form it takes, it's still an idea. One that's unique for each of us.

Oscar Peterson has an idea of home, formed while living the life of a successful jazz pianist travelling the world and seeing all of its possibilities and failings. I'm sure his concept of home has changed over the decades, but I think that one part has remained constant: Canada. There have been times when Canada wasn't as good to Peterson as he's been to it, but this is what defines a patriot: someone who serves and honours their country without expecting anything in return.

The Canadiana Suite is about Peterson's home, Canada. It is an essential piece of Canadian culture to have in your collection, and one of his strongest musical statements. The album expresses his affection and pride for his country and the city where he was born, Montreal. The selections evoke a train ride across Canada. Peterson's father, Daniel, worked as a train porter, and you can imagine him returning from his cross-country travels to tell a young Peterson about the sights he saw.

Many of the songs are blues-based and are a musical tribute to cities and places. The suite moves from east to west. "Ballad to the

East" is a delicate, classically flavoured song about the Maritimes. The majestic "Laurentide Waltz" is about the Laurentian Mountains just north of Montreal. "Place St. Henri" is a swinging tune about the one-time working-class area of Montreal where Peterson grew up. The musical journey moves on to Toronto with Peterson's elegant "Hogtown Blues" and then to Manitoba and Saskatchewan with the two Peterson classics "Blues for the Prairies" and "Wheatland." The frisky "March Past" is about the Calgary Stampede parade, and the suite ends with Peterson's tranquil tribute to the Rocky Mountains, "Land of the Misty Giant." *The Canadiana Suite* is intimate and thoughtful, and Peterson's playing is flawless and elegant.

I once had the pleasure of visiting Peterson at his home. As I approached the house he lived in, I noticed a face carved into the front door. It was pianist Art Tatum's. I couldn't help but smile and think, man, someone special lives here. And when I think of Oscar Peterson, and what his fellow Canadians feel about him, that sums it up. Someone special lives here.

And we should all thank him for that.

■ _____

Limelight Records, #LS 86010

Rahsaan Roland Kirk, 1936–77
I Talk With the Spirits
Recorded in New York City, September 1964

The sax player and flautist Roland Kirk unjustly earned a reputation for being gimmicky because of his eccentric, often bizarre appearance on stage and because he played as many as three instruments in his mouth at once. His stature is worth defending because Kirk was an innovative soloist and an entertaining performer who was well versed in jazz. As a composer, he contributed several important songs, including "Volunteered Slavery," "Serenade to a Cuckoo," and "Bright Moments." Today, DJs around the world plunder his library for new sounds.

Kirk was at home on a number of wind instruments, not just the flute and saxophones, but also nose flute, stritch, manzello, and trumpophone. He was a master of the technique called circular breathing, which meant he could sustain notes for long periods without pausing by exhaling through his mouthpiece while inhaling through his nose. He also modified his saxophones and other instruments so that they could be played simultaneously.

Kirk's achievements are all the more remarkable because, at the age of two, he became blind. He was born Ronald Kirk but after a dream reversed two letters in his first name, and after another dream in 1970, he changed his first name and also adopted the name Rahsaan. As a teenager in the 1950s in Ohio, Kirk played in rhythm and blues bands. He worked as a sideman with Charles Mingus in 1960, but from then on led his own groups. He recorded his first album in 1960, and went on to make twenty-seven more. Sadly he suffered a stroke in 1975 that paralyzed one side of his body. He continued to play and even perform with one hand until his death from another stroke in 1977.

I Talk With the Spirits was recorded for Mercury/Limelight records. Kirk was signed to the label by Quincy Jones (who was then a record executive). He's accompanied by Horace Parlan on piano, Bob Moses on vibes, Michael Fleming on bass, and Walter Perkins on drums, with the occasional assistance of Crystal-Joy Albert on vocals. The two sessions were produced by pianist and songwriter Bobby Scott. Scott would later have success writing "A Taste of Honey," a hit first for the Beatles and later for Herb Alpert and the Tijuana Brass, and "He Ain't Heavy, He's My Brother," which topped the chart for the Hollies.

Of all Kirk's recordings this is his least sensational, a classy collection of ten well-known standards and originals in a variety of moods. It marks the first and only time the multi-instrumentalist played the flute exclusively on a release (a suggestion from his wife). While his contemporaries, such as Herbie Mann, were playing the flute with big round notes, Kirk's sound had more grits and guts to it. The swinging original, "A Quote From Clifford Brown," is a tribute to the trumpet player. "Trees" is a tranquil original that deserves to be better known. Kurt Weill's "My Ship" and the medley "We'll Be Together Again" is soulful and beautiful.

The playful "Serenade to a Cuckoo" is Kirk's best-known song. It was made popular by the British rock band Jethro Tull, whose leader, Ian Anderson, was influenced by Kirk and duplicated his way of singing into his flute as he was playing it. Kirk collected cuckoo clocks and said he got the idea for the song from the cuckoos popping out of their doors to sing when he was rehearsing in his apartment. The cuckoo clock you hear in the song is from his home collection.

■ ────────────────────────────────────

Verve #3145580762

JOHN COLTRANE, 1926–67
A Love Supreme
Recorded in Englewood Cliffs, New Jersey, December 9, 1964

As both a tenor and soprano saxophonist and composer, John Coltrane excelled at pushing himself and expanding the definition of jazz. But, on the surface, it looks unlikely that John Coltrane would be a candidate for fame. From most reports, he was shy and humble, almost apologetic for his gift.

Several of the architects of jazz had considerably longer periods of time to make their contributions to the genre: Duke Ellington lived to be seventy-five, Louis Armstrong to sixty-nine, and Miles Davis died when he was sixty-five. Coltrane's life was much shorter; he died from lung cancer in 1967, a few months short of his forty-first birthday. While his exalted status may have a lot to do with his premature death, you can't understand the development of jazz without looking at Coltrane's career.

He was an accomplished soloist and composer with a sound that was immediately recognizable. Decades after his death, Coltrane's presence can still be found everywhere in jazz. Some of his disciples even named a church after him. At St. John's African Orthodox Church in San Francisco his music is played during the service, and his photo is displayed next to an icon of a black Christ.

Coltrane's creative home for the last stage of his life was Impulse Records. There, Coltrane recorded several radical albums, but not all of his releases are coherent gems that need be in your collection. The most prominent release of the lot, A Love Supreme, still possesses miraculous powers for jazz fans around the world. Inspired by Coltrane's life-changing spiritual awakening in 1957, it was his dedication to God and creation, a spiritual cleansing if you will, presented in four stages of development: "Acknowledgment," "Resolution," "Pursuance," and "Psalm."

Much of the album's cohesiveness comes from the quartet having played together for several years. It is this quartet that is thought of by many to be Coltrane's classic group, with Coltrane on tenor saxophone, pianist McCoy Tyner, Elvin Jones on drums, and bassist Jimmy Garrison. They were all musicians who had their own distinct sound but made a strong contribution to a collaborative group.

A Love Supreme is based on a four-note motif that runs throughout the album. It is most pronounced on "Acknowledgment," the album's first part. From the opening moments, when Elvin Jones bangs a gong (an instrument seldom used in jazz), the message delivered is that this is an album of surprise and spiritual exploration. As "Acknowledgment" becomes established, the motif is played repeatedly in various keys and ends as the group chants the album's title over and over.

Part Two, "Resolution," is a devious band showcase, with Tyner playing a career-defining piano solo, Jones and Garrison providing the rhythmic sparkle, and Coltrane playing his testimony with a ferocious sax solo.

The last two pieces, "Pursuance" and "Psalm," segue into one another as a continuous track. On the former, Coltrane's freesoaring solos are fast and furious as he plays a barrage of notes, managing to transform excess into a virtue. The latter is a prayerlike anthem that is the album's strongest composition. Coltrane's playing is powerfully meditative, with just the slightest touch of a painful wail.

Coltrane's musical journey took people to places they didn't think they could go, and *A Love Supreme* is the most personal statement of his shining career.

■ ───

Impulse! #B000061002

DUKE ELLINGTON, 1899–1974
And His Mother Called Him Bill
Recorded in New York City, August 28 – September 1, 1967

One of the most productive relationships in music, let alone jazz, was the one Duke Ellington had with his musical alter ego, Billy Strayhorn. It is a collaboration that started in 1938 and ended when Strayhorn died in 1967. Their work led to such classics as "Take the A Train," which Strayhorn wrote after listening to Ellington's directions on how to get to his audition, "Daydream," "Star Crossed Lovers," "Satin Doll," and the soundtrack to the movie *Anatomy of a Murder*.

Strayhorn's nickname for Ellington was the Big Monster; Ellington in turn called him the Little Monster or Sweet Pea. Their relationship was so close that, wherever he was in the world, Ellington would call Strayhorn when he had an idea for a song, and they would compose it over the phone. When they had a chance to work together in person, their sessions were often all-night writing marathons, where they would write and sleep in shifts, a musical tag team that alternated throughout the night until they were finished. Their writing styles were so similar that it is impossible to tell where one stopped and the other took over.

Strayhorn was fifty-one when he died on May 31, 1967, after a two-year battle with esophageal cancer. Ellington was devastated and angry, and for the first time in his life didn't want to play. After one concert, a friend found Ellington backstage by himself, with his head hung low, playing Strayhorn's "Lotus Blossom" again and again.

Three months after Strayhorn's death, Ellington and his orchestra were in the studio recording *And His Mother Called Him Bill*, a fifteen-song tribute of material Strayhorn wrote between 1941 and 1967. The album features both well-known and previously unrecorded compositions that show Strayhorn's gift as an arranger and composer.

"Snibor" was written by Strayhorn in 1949 and was titled for a publisher friend whose name it spells backward. It features Johnny Hodges's smooth, swinging saxophone.

"Blood Count" is a song Strayhorn sent from the hospital for a Carnegie Hall concert the orchestra gave in 1967. It is beautifully poignant and features a heartfelt performance by Johnny Hodges. It was Strayhorn's last composition.

"U.M.M.G." stood for the Upper Manhattan Medical Group, the practice of Strayhorn and Ellington's friend and physician Dr. Arthur Logan. It features a beautiful solo played on flugelhorn by Clark Terry.

The solo piano version of "Lotus Blossom" was an afterthought. The band was packing up in the studio when Ellington started reminiscing about the times Strayhorn and he were alone and he would often ask Ellington to play "Lotus Blossom" for him. The tape kept rolling.

Considering all that Strayhorn composed, this album is a fitting tribute. *And His Mother Called Him Bill* is a classic. For those involved, it was an emotionally charged event, a tribute performed with love and understanding.

■

Bluebird RCA #56287

PAUL HORN, b. 1930
Inside the Taj Mahal, Vols. 1 and 11
Recorded in the Taj Mahal, India, April 1968

Unfortunately, the jazz world has largely forgotten Paul Horn, but much of the lack of attention has been his own choice. Horn's an impressive musician, equally at home on the clarinet, flute, and saxophone. Born in New York, Horn grew up in Washington, D.C., and studied at the prestigious Oberlin Conservatory of Music in Ohio, then earned a master's degree at the Manhattan School of Music. After a stint in the army, he played with the Sauter-Finegan big band in New York, then toured and recorded with the Chico Hamilton Quintet from 1956 to 1958. A move to Los Angeles in the early sixties led to the formation of his own group. At the same time he became part of the lucrative session scene and recorded with Duke Ellington, Miles Davis, Quincy Jones, Joni Mitchell, Frank Sinatra, and Buddy Rich. In 1965, he won two Grammy Awards with Lalo Schifrin for the album *Jazz Suite on the Mass Texts*.

In 1966, Horn felt he needed relief from his aggressive pursuit of a career as a jazz musician. He started to search for spiritual fulfilment, which led him to transcendental meditation, and several trips to India to study with the Maharishi Mahesh Yogi.

By 1968, Horn had recorded an impressive fourteen jazz albums, but he still felt there was something lacking. Then, on a trip to India, an artistic transformation occurred when he played the flute inside the Taj Mahal.

The Taj Mahal rests on the south bank of Jumna River outside the city of Agra in India. It was built by the Muslim Mughal

Emperor Shah Jahan in memory of his favourite wife, Arjumand
Bano Begum, who died in 1631 while giving birth to their four-
teenth child. For the next twenty-two years, twenty thousand men
worked to create one of the most beautiful wonders of the world.

The attraction for Horn was the central dome, which is solid
marble and sixty feet in diameter and eighty feet high. The
acoustics are remarkable, and Horn discovered that the dome sus-
pended each note he played on the flute in space, like a natural
reverb or echo, for twenty-eight seconds.

One evening after the tourists left, Horn returned to the Taj
Mahal to make a recording that he intended to give only to friends.
The tape came back sounding better than expected and as more
friends heard it, they suggested he release the recording as an
album. Horn did, the New Age movement embraced *Inside the Taj
Mahal*, and it sold more than one million copies around the world.

For the recording a single mono-microphone was used while
Horn played whatever came in his head. The huge natural reverb
chamber did present some problems. Horn could not play for long
or the notes would come back as a distorted jumble of sounds. So
he played a phrase then waited while the sound settled down, then
played another phrase, until the overlapping echoes were swirling
around in the huge dome.

There were other obstacles, particularly in convincing the Taj
Mahal guard to let him record after closing, and the mosquitoes
were bothersome. Forty-two seconds into the track "Agra," you
can hear them buzzing.

Inside the Taj Mahal is rich with beautiful melodies that relax
and calm, but is it jazz? If the essence of jazz is improvisation, a
spontaneous expression of what the artist feels at the moment,
based on the knowledge and experiences they have acquired over
the years, then the answer is yes.

■————————————————————————

Transparent Music #50008

LENNY BREAU, 1941–84
The Velvet Touch of Lenny Breau Live!
Recorded in Hollywood, September 1968

The guitar player Lenny Breau is one of the most tragic figures in jazz. He is not widely known, neither today nor in his day, but he should have been an international jazz star. Breau's playing was extraordinary, and he often left the impression of playing more than one guitar at the same time. His fans included such guitar masters as Joe Pass, Larry Carlton, George Benson, and Breau's mentor, Chet Atkins. They ranked Breau up there with Charlie Christian and Wes Montgomery as jazz guitar pioneers. His influences were wide and diverse, including flamenco virtuoso Sabicas, guitarist Tal Farlow, fingerstyle country player Chet Atkins, pianist Bill Evans, and saxophonist John Coltrane. In pulling these diverse musical approaches together, Breau created a distinctive sound on the guitar.

Breau fell under the spell of music easily and early. Both his parents, Hal "Lone Pine" Breau and Betty Cody, were country-and-western performers who were often joined on stage by their young guitar-playing son. In 1957, the family moved to Winnipeg, Manitoba, to host a show on CKY Radio.

Breau discovered jazz while listening to a Tal Farlow album and taught himself Farlow's solos by slowing down the record. He was mentored by jazz musicians in Winnipeg and would often rehearse ten or twelve hours a day. In turn, he mentored others, and his friend Randy Bachman remembers many afternoons playing the guitar with Breau, who taught him to play difficult chords and solos. Bachman later used some of what he learned from the jazz solos he played in "Undun" and "Blue Collar," songs he wrote for the Guess Who and Bachman Turner Overdrive.

In 1967, after hearing one of Lenny's tapes, guitarist Chet Atkins, who ran the Nashville office of RCA Victor, signed Breau and the following year produced his first album *The Guitar Sounds of Lenny Breau*. Years later, he cut a duo record with him. Atkins remained a huge fan of Breau's to the end and was a source of emotional support during some difficult years.

In the 1970s, Breau played regularly as a headliner and worked as a sideman for CBC Radio and Television and logged time with Moe Koffman, Beverly Glenn Copland, and Anne Murray. During this time, Breau developed a serious cross-addiction to alcohol and heroin. By mid-decade, the club dates had become more sporadic, and he was widely reputed to be unreliable.

In a 1981 interview with me about his drug addiction, his delicate state was obvious: "It's just one of those things," he said. "It's like, it's like I was hanging out with guys who were doing it. At first, I did it for inspiration, but in the end it turned against me. It's like a seductress. It's like a prostitute who takes more and more and more, and after a while you're spending so much money that you really can't enjoy yourself."

Breau's adult years were nomadic and he lived in Maine, Nashville, New York City, Winnipeg, Toronto, Ottawa, and Edmonton. His last months were spent in a rough part of Los Angeles in the Langham Apartments, a building first owned by Al Jolson and later by Clark Gable. On August 12, 1984, he was found floating face-down in the rooftop swimming pool of the building. The autopsy report said it was death by strangulation. The LAPD believes he was strangled in the seventh-floor apartment he shared with his wife and dumped in the swimming pool. His murder remains unsolved.

Since his death, numerous reissues and new CDs have become available. *The Velvet Touch of Lenny Breau Live!* is the second release of his career. Produced by Danny Davis, the leader of the Nashville

Brass, it was recorded live over a period of two nights in September 1968 at Shelly's Manne-Hole, a short-lived Hollywood jazz club opened by the legendary drummer Shelly Manne. Breau covers a lot of musical ground here, playing blues, flamenco, jazz, and East Indian–flavoured compositions.

Some tracks, such as "Indian Reflections for Ravi" and "Span Jazz" offer glimpses of his brilliance, but they are musical mountains to climb. They are showcases of colossal technique but come up short on cohesive musical ideas. Breau's naked musical sensitivity is endearing, but some of his solos on this album meander and lack focus.

That said, this is still an innovative recording, with Breau often playing chords, melody, and the baseline simultaneously. There are several ways to play the guitar: strum chords; solo by playing single notes with a pick; and finger-style, which consists of plucking the strings either with finger and thumb or with a thumb pick. Breau's gift was that he could do all three, all at the same time, and sound like three guitar players.

On the CD, Breau performs solos on electric and acoustic guitars, and in a trio with two of his friends from Winnipeg, Ron Halldorson (on bass) and Reg Kelln (on drums). On "No Greater Love," "Mercy, Mercy," "A Taste of Honey," and "Bluesette," Breau's playing is dazzling and polished. These tracks tip the scale, making this an essential album. They show a risk-taker in action, a guitarist who lands on his feet no matter how high he jumps.

■ ──

One Way Records #29315

QUINCY JONES, b. 1933
Walking in Space
Recorded in Englewood Cliffs, New Jersey, June 19, 1969

Quincy Jones's story is extraordinary. He started in the 1950s as a jazz musician playing the trumpet and as a freelance arranger and became a mogul and one of the most sought-after record producers in the world. He has defied the boundary lines for music genres because he sees it as a whole.

In August 1974, Jones suffered a near-fatal cerebral aneurysm – the bursting of blood vessels leading to the brain. Jones required two delicate operations and six months of recuperation. Unfortunately, staples left permanently in his skull made it impossible for him to play any more. But Jones probably would not have had the impact he has had on music if he had remained a trumpet player.

His list of credentials is highly impressive: He produced the biggest-selling album in the world, Michael Jackson's *Thriller*, and the largest single, "We Are the World." He has worked with Peggy Lee, George Benson, Dinah Washington, Paul Simon, Billie Holiday, Count Basie, Dizzy Gillespie, Miles Davis, Frank Sinatra, Duke Ellington, Donna Summer, Diana Ross, Aretha Franklin, Lionel Hampton, and Leslie Gore, among many, many others. Jones has been nominated for seventy-six Grammys and has won twenty-six times. He wrote the theme music for the television shows *Sanford and Son*, *Ironside*, and *The Cosby Show*. He's written thirty-four film scores for such movies as *The Getaway*, *The Pawnbroker*, the 1967 version of *In Cold Blood*, and *In the Heat of the Night*.

Jones has achieved so much in part by starting at an early age, which he did as a means of escaping a brutally hard childhood. He was just twenty-three and newly in New York when he recorded his first album, *This Is How I Feel About Jazz*, for Verve. It comprises six tracks, each with a strong identity, featuring, among others, Art Farmer, Charles Mingus, Milt Jackson, Phil Woods, Hank Jones, Zoot Sims, and Herbie Mann in the orchestra. It was a strong contender for the essential Quincy Jones album to own.

In 1969, Quincy Jones was thirty-six and still driven. He'd scored twelve movies in five years and wanted to go back into the studio, where there would be no film monitors to watch and images to play along with, to record a jazz album with some of his favourite musicians. It was a return to the idea of arranging and conducting a band, much the way Jones started in music by writing arrangements for the big bands of Duke Ellington, Count Basie, and Tommy Dorsey. Producer Creed Taylor also thought it was a good idea and signed him to his label, CTI.

The musical tone for the album was rock and rhythm and blues played on electric instruments and incorporated into the context of a big band. It was a strange musical mix that worked. *Walking in Space* received two Grammy Awards and a four-and-a-half-star review from *Down Beat*.

In his usual fashion, Jones attracted some of the best musicians to appear on his comeback jazz album. They included trombonist J.J. Johnson, trumpeter Freddie Hubbard, flautists Roland Kirk and Hubert Laws, Bob James on electric piano, Toots Thielemans on harmonica and guitar, Ray Brown on electric bass, drummer Grady Tate, and Eric Gale on electric guitar. The album was recorded and engineered by Rudy Van Gelder at his studio in Englewood Cliffs, New Jersey. Over the last forty years, Van Gelder's studio has been the birthplace of many of the classic jazz albums.

At Creed Taylor's suggestion, the first two selections, "Dead End" and "Walking in Space" are from the musical *Hair*, which was playing on Broadway. "Dead End" opens perfectly with a walking bass line by Ray Brown, then just a touch of guitar from Eric Gale, leading to full-blown brass and reeds. At the end, Brown improvises a beautiful bass solo that serves as a segue to "Walking in Space." On this cut, Freddie Hubbard solos on trumpet with an authentic bebop sensibility and Roland Kirk plays reeds with a jolt of pure inspiration.

The musical centrepiece of the album is Quincy's arrangement of "Killer Joe." It was written by Benny Golson, his former bandmate in the Dizzy Gillespie orchestra. The song features delicious solos by Hubert Laws on flute and Freddie Hubbard on trumpet but, because of the way the song is mixed, the driving force behind it is Ray Brown's thumping bass.

Jones's arrangement of brass and reeds was innovative at the time and exceedingly polished, and since has become his trademark. He has a knack for setting the right tempo for a song. Musicians who have played on his sessions say that, as a conductor and arranger, Jones helps them raise the bar because his strength lies in making everyone feel special and valued.

■ ──

Verve #3145434992

CHICK COREA, b. 1941

Return to Forever and *Light as a Feather*

Recorded in London, England, February and October 1972

If you ever want a quick understanding of what jazz-rock sounds like, then the music of Return to Forever is a good place to start. It was, in its early years, a hugely innovative and influential jazz fusion group.

Return to Forever was the brainchild of Chick Corea, who has built his reputation on never being pigeonholed. Corea had been a part of Miles Davis's jazz rock exploration in the late 1960s, appearing on Davis's seminal albums *Bitches Brew* and *In a Silent Way.* Fusion or jazz rock was seen at the time as an opportunity for innovative jazz musicians to explore the use of many of the electric instruments used by rock groups, such as Genesis and Emerson, Lake and Palmer, and in the process appeal to a larger audience. Corea understood the music but brought to it the considerable jazz knowledge he had acquired playing with a wide range of musicians, including Stan Getz, Mongo Santamaria, Blue Mitchell, and Sarah Vaughan.

There were three versions of Return to Forever who made eight albums that were recorded for three labels. The first version of the band (1972–73) included Corea on electric piano, veteran jazz musician Joe Farrell on sax and flutes, Stanley Clarke on bass, Brazilian percussionist Airto Moreira on drums and percussion, and his wife, Flora Purim, on vocals.

Their second release, *Light as a Feather*, was recorded for Polydor in October 1972 in London, England, while the group was appearing at Ronnie Scott's Jazz Club. The album is an explosion of melodies, rhythmic sparkles, and sounds. One of the drawbacks of the fusion movement in jazz was that a good deal of the music was a monotonous groove. On *Light as a Feather*, melody is king.

"You're Everything" has a calm, catchy opening, featuring Corea playing solo on the Fender Rhodes electric piano, then it goes into double time with percussion, bass, and flute joining in. Purim's Brazilian accent brings an icy detachment to the music that is sexy and enticing. The title song, "Light as a Feather," is a tour de force that highlights Purim, Corea, and Farrell. Farrell's performance on flute is assured and confident and raises the question why he never became better known. "Captain Marvel," which Corea wrote for Stan Getz, has a strong samba melody and once again features a breath-busting performance on the flute by Farrell.

The album's greatest moment occurs on the closing track, "Spain." Of the many songs Corea has composed, this is his best known and has become a regular part of the jazz repertoire. It is a majestic, melodic nine-minute rhapsody.

Light as a Feather has liquid electricity running throughout. A good portion of this energy originates with Corea, whose performance is stunning and provides insight into why he is one of the most celebrated pianists of his generation. He is an in-the-moment improviser whose compositions have a melodic grace and power. His playing shows he has the virtuosity to take his considerable talent in any direction he wants.

■

Universal #9266

JOE PASS, 1929–94
Virtuoso
Recorded in Los Angeles, December 1973

Virtuosity is a word subject to much interpretation, yet it boils down to being one of the best at playing your instrument. To achieve virtuosity is a painstaking and time-consuming process that demands ability, technique, style, and sweat. Joe Pass, called by some "the president of bebop guitar," was a virtuoso of the highest order, and by using the raw material of experience, perseverance, and inspiration he became one of the best at playing his instrument, the guitar.

Joseph Anthony Passalaqua was born in New Brunswick, New Jersey, to a non-musical family. The family moved to Johnstown, Pennsylvania, where Joe started to play guitar at age nine, encouraged by his father. For five years he practised at least six hours a day. He turned to jazz after hearing Charlie Parker, and initially toured with small bands. But it was a difficult journey for Pass, and at one point it looked as if he might not make it. There were hurdles to overcome: a ten-year addiction to heroin and four years in prison for narcotics offences in the 1950s.

By 1962, Pass had kicked the habit, and in 1963, he received *Down Beat* magazine's New Star Award. He moved to Los Angeles but worked in muddy obscurity as a sideman for much of the 1960s, with the exception of time spent touring with George Shearing and Benny Goodman. Oscar Peterson heard him play in the early 1970s, and brought him to the attention of Norman Granz, who promptly recruited Pass as the house guitarist for his new jazz label, Pablo. Pass toured and recorded in a variety of

settings, ranging from solo and duo to small ensembles with Oscar
Peterson, Ella Fitzgerald, Duke Ellington, Sarah Vaughan, Dizzy
Gillespie, Milt Jackson, and Zoot Sims.

Pass's most significant and popular contributions were the
albums he recorded under his own name. His first release for
Pablo was *Virtuoso*, and it made him a star. Recorded in 1973, it
features Pass playing solo eleven standards and one original song.
Pass's selections are tasteful and imaginative: classics from the
great songwriters – Cole Porter's "Night and Day," Jerome Kern's
"All Things You Are," Jimmy Van Heusen's "Here's That Rainy
Day," and Ray Noble's "Cherokee." These songs set the tone for
the album, which outsold everything else put out by Pablo.

At the time of *Virtuoso*'s release solo jazz albums were primarily the domain of pianists. In 1973, guitarists were more focused
on heavy-handed jazz rock and *Virtuoso* provided some much-
needed relief, a long sonic sigh, if you will. Pass's playing was
about timing, harmony, and the use of space and silence.

Pass set new standards for solo guitar. His playing is worth
pausing over because it was elegant and extraordinary. He was a
sensitive player but one who could swing as though he were the
entire group. *Virtuoso* was the foundation upon which the salad
days of the rest of Pass's career were built. He was everything the
title implies, a virtuoso.

■ ——————————————————————————————————

Pablo #23107082

PHIL NIMMONS, b. 1923
Atlantic Suite/Suite P.E.I./Tributes
Recorded in Toronto, August 1973 and June 1975

More than anything else in clarinet virtuoso Phil Nimmons's lengthy list of impressive accomplishments, this 1996 Sackville re-release of his 1975 recording of his (and the jazz world's) beloved *Atlantic Suite* attests to his enduring love of both his country and jazz music. In this double-CD collection, *Atlantic Suite* is paired with an earlier recording of *Suite P.E.I.*, in a fond tribute to the beauty of Canada's eastern provinces.

In 1945, Nimmons left home in Vancouver to study at Juilliard and later at the Toronto Conservatory of Music, where his teachers and peers dubbed him "the jazzer" because, even then, he was a staunch champion of the music he loved more than any other. "I've *always* been the jazzer," he told writer Mark Miller for his book *Boogie, Pete & the Senator*. "I'm *still* going through the process of trying to convince my friends that this is music, too."

His friends weren't the only people he never wearied of trying to persuade that jazz was a significant genre of music. In 1951, he became a founding member of the Canadian League of Composers, along with the composers of some of the country's best-known contemporary music. Miller reports that Nimmons alone took the CLC's activist stance into the realm of jazz. And he didn't stop there. He proudly used his position at the CBC, where he wrote and performed for more than twenty years, to lobby management at every opportunity on behalf of the jazz industry. To this day he continues to devote himself to jazz education and still works for the greater recognition of and performance opportunities for Canadian jazz musicians.

Phil Nimmons is widely acknowledged as "the elder statesman of jazz" in Canada. A performer, arranger, educator, clinician, and artistic director of music programs, he is also the composer of more than four hundred original contemporary classical and jazz compositions for stage, television, radio, and film, in addition to hundreds of jazz orchestrations. His bands, Nimmons 'N' Nine and the later Nimmons 'N' Nine Plus Six, performed for decades on radio and television and concert stages across the country. He has been accorded nearly every relevant Canadian honour and never appears anywhere without his Officer of the Order of Canada pin prominently displayed on his lapel.

But for good fortune – and some nimble footwork on Nimmons's part – the 1970s tour of the Atlantic provinces that inspired his crowning *Atlantic Suite* might never have happened. Almost all of the regular band members of Nimmons 'N' Nine Plus Six were tied up with studio gigs, so he was forced to put together a fresh ensemble – an exciting blend of young talent and experienced solo voices, such as trumpeter Herbie Spanier and tenor-sax player Art Ellefson. They're all at their Nimmons-led best on this recording of *Atlantic Suite*, which won the Juno for best jazz record in 1976, the first year the Junos included jazz as an award category.

In his liner notes, Farley Mowat says, "I was so delighted by the images Nimmons conjures up in the *Atlantic Suite* that I couldn't resist the impulse to tell others what I had seen, smelled, felt, and heard in them." Nimmons has divided his *Atlantic Suite* tour de force into four distinct movements. The first movement is entitled "Harbours," which Mowat says represents "the beginning and the end of man's encroachment on the sea. . . . In this movement one of the greatest of the world's harbours, Halifax and Bedford Basin, comes alive in all of its intricate melding of ageless mysteries and modern mechanical miracles, old voices and new."

The second movement is "Islands," written "under the spell of Prince Edward Island . . . a strange marriage between land and water," followed by "Tides," a story "of power beyond our understanding," and finally, "Horizons," which "returns us to the people of the sea, the Newfoundlanders."

Nimmons's love affair with Prince Edward Island began some years earlier, a cherished relationship he turned into the seventeen-minute "Suite P.E.I.," recorded by Nimmons 'N' Nine at Toronto's Canadian National Exhibition in 1973. *Tributes*, big band songs he recorded in 1979, comprises the second disc in the set and features virtuoso performances by a band made up of legends, including Nimmons in top form on the clarinet, Guido Basso, Rob McConnell, Moe Koffman, Ed Bickert, Don Thompson, and others.

■ _____

Sackville Recordings #5003

KEITH JARRETT, b. 1945
The Köln Concert
Recorded in Köln, Germany, January 24, 1975

The piano has played a pivotal role in the development of jazz, and pianists have created many of the genre's major innovations. Keith Jarrett is one such player. He started playing at age three and studied the classical repertoire until his late teens, when he turned to jazz. He started out playing bebop, first with the Charles Lloyd Quartet, and in 1970–71, he played electric piano with Miles Davis. He then formed a trio with Charlie Haden and Paul Motian, which became a quartet in 1972, when tenor saxophonist Dewey Redman joined. The group disbanded in 1976. From then until 1983, he played only solo and only acoustic. Today, he suffers from chronic fatigue syndrome and rarely performs.

Jarrett is a giant of what is called post-bop and a musical genius who takes substantial risks. Many of his most celebrated recordings are his solo piano efforts, where he has played without the safety net of sidemen. Don Heckman, the jazz critic for the *Los Angeles Times*, put it aptly when he wrote, "Keith Jarrett's piano playing is based upon one fundamental tenet: no fear."

The no-fear factor played a role in *The Köln Concert*, the most celebrated of all of the recordings Keith Jarrett has made. The night before the concert, Jarrett played in Lausanne then found that he couldn't sleep. Despite his weariness, early the next morning he made the long drive to Köln.

When Jarrett arrived at his hotel he was exhausted. He checked in but still couldn't sleep. He went to the sound check, only to find an inadequate piano and, to make matters worse, there was not enough time to replace it with one that met Jarrett's specifications. He returned to his hotel to relax, but still couldn't fall asleep. Jarrett and his producer from the ECM label, Manfred Eicher, with whom he was travelling, went to an Italian restaurant for dinner. Jarrett started sweating profusely from the excessive heat in the crowded restaurant. The service was extremely slow and their meal arrived just fifteen minutes before Jarrett had to be at the venue.

Given the day's events, Jarrett and Eicher wondered if it was pointless to record the concert that night. But, with such short notice, they'd still have to pay for the engineer and gear, so they decided to proceed with the recording. They figured that at least they would have a document of the event to analyze.

As Jarrett slowly walked out on stage that night he started to fall asleep, but the moment he sat down at the piano his fatigue disappeared. He played one extended improvised song that he composed on the spot.

As Jarrett and Eicher finished the remainder of the tour, they listened to the cassette in the car. They had some reservations about the quality of the recording, but they both recognized that Jarrett's playing was inspired. The music he made that night is one of the great pleasures of jazz. It covered a wide range of emotion: sometimes sombre and meditative, sometimes frantic, and always elegant. He did a masterful job of adapting to the piano's limitations and played with warmth and friendliness. You can hear him coming up with ideas, marking time until inspiration hits. His performance took piano improvisation to new heights.

The Köln Concert, which has sold more than three million copies since its release, is one of the best-selling jazz albums of all time.

■ ───

ECM #1064

JIM HALL, b. 1930
Concierto
Recorded in Englewood Cliffs, New Jersey, April 1975

Jim Hall is the latter-day patron saint of jazz guitar. He plays with a jeweller's touch, a purity of tone, and says more with fewer notes then anyone else in jazz. When he plays, Hall sounds just like he does in person: warm, intimate, humble, and mellow. He is the personification of style and elegance in jazz. He has influenced several generations of guitar players, including Bill Frisell and Pat Metheny.

Hall was born in Buffalo, New York, and as a child heard electric-guitar pioneer Charlie Christian play on a Benny Goodman recording. He was hooked, and from that point forward he sought out the music. With the exception of a period in California in the 1950s, he has been a mainstay of the New York City jazz scene. He and his wife, Jane, and their dog, Django, live near the Village.

Hall is a versatile player who has recorded almost forty CDs under his own name. As a studio musician in the 1960s, Hall held down the much sought-after guitar chair in the house band on *The Merv Griffin Show*. He has recorded with Stan Getz, Pat Metheny, Jimmy Giuffre, Chico Hamilton, and Bob Brookmeyer. It is Jim Hall's guitar you hear playing along with Ella Fitzgerald on her charming live rendition of "Mack the Knife." Hall played on the pivotal Sonny Rollins album *The Bridge* and played with Paul Desmond on several of his albums. He made two award-winning duets albums with pianist Bill Evans.

One of Hall's most acclaimed albums is the classic *Concierto* from 1975. It features an all-star band with Chet Baker on trumpet,

Paul Desmond on alto sax, Roland Hanna on piano, Ron Carter on bass, and Steve Gadd on drums. The arrangement is by Don Sebesky. *Concierto* was first released on producer Creed Taylor's imprint label, CTI. Since its initial release, it has come out in various forms, with several alternate takes included as a bonus. CTI declared bankruptcy in the early 1980s, and today the master tapes are owned by Sony BMG Music Entertainment.

Ellington and Strayhorn's "Rock Skippin'," Cole Porter's "You'd Be So Nice to Come Home To," and wife Jane Hall's "The Answer Is Yes" are strong, firm contributions to the album. Hall's dry, less-is-more approach to playing the guitar understates the imagination and intelligence found in his playing.

Concierto's focal point though is Spanish composer Juan Rodrigo's 1939 *Concierto de Arjanuez*. Hall initially didn't want to record it, as Miles Davis's 1960 orchestral version was considered the definitive version. He was won over by Don Sebesky's imaginative, nineteen-minute arrangement that recasts the song for a small group.

It helps that Hall had two important, brilliant stylists playing on the album, Desmond and Baker, two players sonically sympathetic to Hall's sound. Their solos are melodically mature and precise. No one disappoints, especially not Hall. He knows how to turn ideas, ability, and know-how into compelling music.

■ ――――――――――――――――――――――――――――――

Columbia/Legacy #65132

TONY BENNETT, b. 1926 / BILL EVANS, 1929–80
The Tony Bennett/Bill Evans Album
Recorded in Berkeley, California, June 1975

It was jazz singer Annie Ross who first proposed pairing the singer's singer Tony Bennett with Bill Evans, the most emotionally evocative pianist of them all. There was just one problem: Evans almost always worked alone. In his autobiography, Bennett says he was surprised when Ross suggested the collaboration because Evans rarely recorded with singers, and he was even more surprised when Bill Evans liked the idea. Bill Evans said later, as quoted in Peter Pettinger's book *Bill Evans: How My Heart Sings*, "It was one of the ideas that was in the air for years. I always figured that if Tony would do one of my tunes, I'd be overjoyed. I like Tony's singing. To me, he is one of those guys that keep developing – digging deeper into their resources."

As Bennett tells it in his book, *The Good Life*, "Bill Evans was there when I sang with Dave Brubeck at the all-star concert on the White House lawn in 1962. By the sixties, especially after his tenure with the Miles Davis Sextet and his own groundbreaking trio, Bill had become the most-listened-to jazz pianist in the world. Bill happened to be playing in London at Ronnie Scott's, so John Bunch (Bennett's long-time pianist) and I went down to hear Bill's latest trio, which impressed us mightily. My original idea was to make an album with my voice and two pianos . . . Bill Evans and John Bunch, but John discouraged me saying it would be better with Bill Evans alone."

Tony hadn't recorded accompanied by just a piano in nearly two decades, and Bill was accustomed to having a bass and drummer, so both of them were working without a musical safety net. Before the recording dates, Evans suggested that Tony keep his musicians at home and he would do the same. He wanted as few distractions as possible, to ensure it was an intimate experience, so throughout the recording only one engineer, Evans and Bennett, and Evans's manager, Helen Keane, were in the studio. It was a wise decision that resulted in this, the first of two exceptional albums.

All of the songs on this album – like almost everything Tony Bennett has sung throughout his career – are right up there on any list of all-time favourites. Evans's "Waltz for Debby," written for his niece, is one of this album's highlights. "My Foolish Heart," "Some Other Time," and his thrilling treatment of Johnny Burke and Jimmy Van Heusen's "But Beautiful" give a nostalgic new dimension to these beautiful jazz standards. Everything here lives up to the philosophy Bennett learned from Count Basie after working with the Basie band at Birdland in the 1950s: Keep it simple and swinging.

Although Tony Bennett has been regarded as a superstar pop singer for decades, he has always shown a deep reverence for jazz music, using jazz players in all of his performances and recording sessions. In Bennett's book, *The Good Life*, an interviewer is quoted as asking Bill Evans whether what he and Bennett had achieved on this CD could be called a jazz sound. Evans answered, "As far as I'm concerned, it is. This is one of the prime experiences of my life. Every great jazz musician I know idolizes Tony. From Philly Joe Jones to Miles Davis, you name it. The reason is that Tony is a great musical artist. He puts music first, and has dedicated himself to it. He has great respect for music and musicians and this comes through. It's a joy to work with somebody like that. To me, that's music."

I'm with him.

■ ————————————————————————

Fantasy/Concord #9489

PAUL DESMOND, 1924–77
The Paul Desmond Quartet Live
Recorded in Toronto, October–November 1975

Paul Desmond possessed one of the most instantly recognizable
sounds in jazz. He once described his light, airy tone on the alto
sax as sounding like a dry martini. Charlie Parker said Desmond
was one of his favourite sax players. That's high praise indeed.

He was born Paul Emil Breitenfeld but changed his last name
by randomly picking a new one from the San Francisco telephone
book. He started playing the alto sax in 1943, the same year he
joined the army, playing with the 253 AGF band stationed in San
Francisco. During this time, he was introduced to Dave Brubeck,
who was on his way overseas as a rifleman. After the war, the two
met up again, and for seventeen years starting in 1951, Desmond
was the alto saxophonist in one of the most successful jazz groups
ever, the Dave Brubeck Quartet. It was Desmond who wrote the
Quartet's biggest hit, "Take Five." After the Quartet disbanded in
1967, Desmond did not play in public for three years, until friends
coaxed him to play occasional gigs. One of those gigs was in
Toronto, at the now-defunct Bourbon Street club, where *The Paul
Desmond Quartet Live* was recorded in the fall of 1975.

Desmond received an appealing offer to play the club. He
asked his friend guitarist Jim Hall to play the gig but he wasn't
available. Hall recommended Toronto guitarist Ed Bickert. The
rest of the group was rounded out with two other Canadians, Don
Thompson on bass and Jerry Fuller on drums. It was thanks to

Thompson, a first-rate musician and audiophile, that the gigs at Bourbon Street were recorded. He brought in his own recording gear and let the tape roll. The record company bought the rights to use those tapes.

The Paul Desmond Quartet Live is a refined album with no overstatement or glibness. The music is at times moody but always cool and never limp. The selections include classics such as Antonio Carlos Jobim's "Wave," "My Funny Valentine," by Rodgers and Hart, Van Heusen's "Nancy," and Gerry Mulligan's "Line For Lyons."

Desmond's musical relationship with the other players is so comfortable you can hear the songs evolve as they are being played. Desmond's best-known composition, "Take Five," is a musical tour de force. Bickert and Thompson improvise with an exotic scale that reminded the group of the Middle East. During one solo, Desmond is said to have remarked to Thompson, "I can smell the camels from here." From then on, they jokingly referred to the song as "The Camel" and not "Take Five."

This recording is a high point of Desmond's post-Brubeck years. Fifteen months later in New York City, in February 1977, he played his last concert. By then, he needed two or three breaths to complete phrases that in the past would have been effortless. He had lung cancer. Paul Desmond died on May 30, 1977.

■ ———————————————————————————————————

A&M #543501

JIMMY ROWLES, 1918–96
Stan Getz Presents Jimmy Rowles: The Peacocks
Recorded in New York City, October 1975

Pianist Jimmy Rowles earned his stripes accompanying many of the best singers in jazz: Peggy Lee, Frank Sinatra, Julie London, Billie Holiday, Carmen McRae, Tony Bennett, and Sarah Vaughan. They all enjoyed working with him because he seemed to come up with the perfect chord for any situation, he could anticipate what they were going to do, and his piano playing never got in the way. In his later years, Rowles used some of the knowledge he acquired to help developing artists. When Diana Krall decided to incorporate singing with her playing, it was at Rowles's urging while she was studying with him in Los Angeles.

As a young man, Rowles was crazy for Guy Lombardo and his pianist, Freddie Kreitzer. After hearing a record by the Benny Goodman Trio, when Teddy Wilson was the piano player in the group, Rowles's life changed. He started playing like Wilson and quit law school to devote himself to music. In time, Rowles worked with Slim and Slam, Lester Young, and the big bands of Benny Goodman, Woody Herman, Tommy Dorsey, and Les Brown.

In the 1950s, his versatility and ability to read music quickly made him an A-list session musician. He appeared on many records and film scores. It is Rowles who can be heard on Henry Mancini's "Baby Elephant Walk," from the 1962 movie *Hatari*. The film studios thought so highly of Rowles he became Marilyn Monroe's singing coach. His best-known composition, "The

Peacocks," was used in Bertrand Tavernier's 1986 film *'Round Midnight.*

When Rowles played the piano, he used to rub an adhesive coating called Tacky Finger into his fingertips so they wouldn't slip off the piano keys. The idea came to Rowles when he was in line at the bank and saw the teller rubbing the substance into her fingers so she could count the money.

Rowles was an underrated stylist and an affable man who was loved by singers and musicians alike and was nominated for a Grammy six times. One of his best albums was made possible because of his friend and old bandmate from Woody Herman's Thundering Herd, Stan Getz. Getz had a deal with Columbia Records that enabled him to release records by other artists. In 1975, he took Rowles into a New York City studio and recorded *Stan Getz Presents Jimmy Rowles: The Peacocks*, showcasing Rowles as pianist, songwriter, and soloist, with a quartet and in duets with Getz. There are thirteen pieces, including originals and standards. It is a beautiful record from start to finish.

"The Peacocks" is the achingly beautiful title song for the album. It is a soft, evocative duet with Getz. The song came to Rowles one night when he was driving home from work. He pulled over to the side of the road and wrote down what he had been thinking and finished the song the next day.

"What Am I Here For?" was a question posed by Duke Ellington in 1942 when he wrote this song. The second Ellington composition, "Serenade to Sweden," was inspired by the warm reception Ellington received when he toured the country in 1939. Both are gorgeous melodies played by Rowles and Getz.

"I'll Never Be the Same" is a bittersweet rendition of a song Billie Holiday sang in the thirties with saxophonist Lester Young. Al Jolson's "My Buddy" is a poignant masterpiece. Both songs feature Rowles on vocals (he sounds like Miles Davis with laryngitis) and gently reveal the melancholy heart of a ballad.

Rowles's solo rendition of "Body and Soul" is unpredictable and very satisfying. He has a deep understanding of jazz piano and you can hear traces of Teddy Wilson, Art Tatum, and Earl Hines.

■ —————————————————————————————————————

Sony BMG #52975

GARY BURTON, b. 1943
Dreams So Real
Recorded in Ludwigsburg, Germany, December 1975

Vibraphonist virtuoso Gary Burton, who grew up in a small
farming community in Indiana, is today one of the central figures
in modern jazz. He has had a dual career as a performer and as a
teacher. As dean of curriculum and later executive vice president
at the Berklee College of Music in Boston (he retired in 2004), he
has had a hand in shaping many of the great musical minds of the
past thirty years.

As a performer, his career has spanned four decades. He was a
precocious child who taught himself the vibraphone by playing to
Miles Davis and Dave Brubeck records. Today he is recognized as
one of the top four-mallet vibraphonists in the world. He recorded
his first album when he was seventeen with Chet Atkins and Hank
Garland. He has received five Grammy Awards, and has played
with pianist George Shearing and saxophonist Stan Getz, both of
whom understood how to engage an audience by playing the
melody. He recorded and toured as a duo with pianist Chick Corea
and led his own group. His influences have been Bill Evans, Miles
Davis, Sonny Rollins, and to a great extent, Corea.

Burton was the first important jazz figure to employ guitarist
Pat Metheny, who joined Burton's band when he was nineteen.
Metheny has said that he not only learned about music from
Burton but also about the business side of music.

Dreams So Real was recorded in December 1975 for the prestigious ECM label. It features Burton in a quintet, with Metheny

and Mick Goodrick on guitars, Bob Moses on drums, and Steve Swallow on bass.

There are eight compositions here, each showcasing the writing of Carla Bley, an eccentric figure in jazz who is underappreciated as a composer. Burton was one of the first to recognize her talent in 1967, when he recorded an album of her songs, *A Genuine Tong Funeral*.

The title song, "Dreams So Real," is energetic, and Burton's fluid and buoyant playing makes his four mallets sound like two. "Ictus/Syndrome" is a rhythmically propulsive gem. "Jesus Maria" is dazzling but in a subdued, understated way. "Vox Humana" is a beautiful, unpredictable melody that borders on being free and abstract.

Gary Burton is a magnificent stylist who sees the vibes as a kind of keyboard and uses every opportunity to play chords and multiple lines. He has strong melodic phrasing and good theme development. *Dreams So Real* is a gem of an album, clearly driven by musical intelligence.

■ _____

ECM #1072

WEATHER REPORT, 1970–86
Heavy Weather
Recorded in Hollywood, 1977

Weather Report was one of the most dazzling, influential, prominent, ingenious, and critically acclaimed ensembles in jazz, and is considered one of the most influential jazz-rock groups. Its creative fulcrum was the two founding members, keyboardist Joe Zawinul and saxophonist Wayne Shorter.

The two first met in 1958 when they were members of the Maynard Ferguson big band. Zawinul became the pianist for singer Dinah Washington and then the Cannonball Adderley group, where he composed their biggest hits, "Country Preacher" and "Mercy, Mercy, Mercy." After Shorter's tenure with Ferguson, he joined the hard-bop group, Art Blakey and the Jazz Messengers, and then the second edition of the Miles Davis Quintet, where he was Davis's most prolific composer.

The Shorter and Zawinul paths crossed again when they both appeared on Davis's cutting-edge album, *In a Silent Way*. (The title track is a Zawinul composition.) It is not certain if the Davis incubator provided the creative spark for Weather Report but it is safe to assume that they found Davis's innovative use of rock rhythms and electric instruments both enjoyable and challenging to play.

They formed Weather Report in late 1970. The group's name came from Shorter who thought it the best way to describe a band whose sound changed from day to day, like the weather. Their sound did shift and evolve. Initially a co-operative effort between the principals, in time it became more a group that showcased Zawinul's compositions and his wide array of keyboards and electronics.

Of the seventeen albums recorded by Weather Report, several are gems but the one that consistently shows up on "best of" lists is *Heavy Weather*. It was released just as the jazz-rock era was drawing to a close but showed there was still some life to the music.

It contained remarkable songs that defy categorization, skilfully and imaginatively played under the watchful eye of Zawinul, who was never short of confidence or a point of view. "Birdland," his tribute to the big bands of the 1950s, was named after the New York jazz club where he and Shorter first met. The song is infectious, and its crossover popularity helped move Weather Report out of jazz clubs into large soft-seaters. The Manhattan Transfer and Maynard Ferguson also had considerable success with their versions of the song, which provided Zawinul with substantial song-writing royalties. The beautiful ballad "A Remark You Made" is another classic by Zawinul, featuring Shorter's haunting soprano sax.

Shorter's contributions, both as player and composer, are fleeting, but he does show us his composing chops on "Harlequin" and "Palladium." His moments on soprano and tenor saxophone are juicy and flawless, resting on top of the multilayered sound of the ensemble.

Heavy Weather's musical bright light was the fretless bassist Jaco Pastorius, a recent addition to the group. His contribution to its overall sound was enormous. His dazzling solos, particularly in the higher register, were a good contrast to the at-times heavy-bottomed sound of Weather Report. Pastorius's glorious "Teen Town," which was named after a youth centre in Fort Lauderdale, Florida, is played with drive, funk, and fire. A genius on the electric, fretless bass, he was a sad, tragic figure who died in 1987 at the age of thirty-five from injuries sustained in a fight with a club manager in Florida.

Weather Report never produced another record as influential and as popular as *Heavy Weather*, and the group disbanded that year.

∎

Sony BMG #65108

◼

PETE CHRISTLIEB/WARNE MARSH QUINTET
Pete Christlieb, b. 1945, Warne Marsh, 1927–87
Apogee
Recorded in Los Angeles, 1977, released 1978

In 1977, Walter Becker and Donald Fagen, the duo at the core of the rock band Steely Dan, were at the height of their popularity with the release of their sonic masterpiece, *Aja*. The jazz-drenched album featured blistering solos played by several of Los Angeles' best session players. One of them was tenor saxophonist Pete Christlieb, who was featured prominently on the track "Deacon Blues." Following the release of *Aja*, Becker and Fagen produced *Apogee*, an album Christlieb recorded with his friend and teacher, tenor saxophonist Warne Marsh.

At the time, Pete Christlieb, who had earlier played jazz with Buddy Rich and Louis Bellson, was a member of the Tonight Show Band with Doc Severinsen. He was also a popular studio rock musician and had played on sessions with Tom Waits, Quincy Jones, the Fifth Dimension, and Rita Coolidge. A major musical turning point for Christlieb was meeting Warne Marsh at a rehearsal for a big band they were both members of in Los Angeles.

Marsh became a musical mentor of sorts to Christlieb. He had played music in the Army and later studied with the gifted, blind pianist Lennie Tristano. Marsh taught music from time to time and played with Supersax, a five-sax nonet dedicated to playing the solos of Charlie Parker. Marsh's recognition was slow in coming, but his playing was often praised by musicians in the know, such as Wayne Shorter and Bill Evans. Just before Christmas of 1987, at age sixty, Marsh collapsed and died mid-song at an L.A. jazz club called Dante's.

Apogee is a major jazz album that was unavailable from the 1980s until its release on CD in the spring of 2004. It features both Christlieb and Marsh on tenor saxophones. The album has the feeling of a musical prize fight or duel, but it also has the sound of two friends who inspire each other conversing. Marsh (who was fifty-one) sounds the most mature musically and delivers beautifully executed ideas. Christlieb (who was thirty-three) is an imaginative soloist whose musical diversity shines through. Together they made a beautiful team.

Joe Roccianso, who had been living in Christlieb's garage apartment, wrote some great charts for the session and contributed the album's all-out burner, "Tenors of the Time."

Marsh chose "317 E 32nd," a song by his former teacher, Lennie Tristano. "Rapunzel," by Walter Becker and Donald Fagen, is compositionally one of the strongest songs on the CD.

Apogee is a remarkable and vigorous album. It will never go out of style because its hard bebop sound, an energetic exercise in pushing the boundaries of improvisation, is one of the cornerstones of jazz.

■ _____

Warner Bros #BSR3236

⊡

PAT METHENY, b. 1954
The Pat Metheny Group
Recorded in Oslo, Norway, January 1978

Pat Metheny is one of the most popular musicians in modern jazz. He's recorded highly regarded trio albums, Grammy Award–winning solo albums, scores for motion pictures, collaborations with the composers Steve Riech and Ornette Coleman, and duets with fellow guitarists John Scofield and Charlie Haden. His most successful work has been with the band he formed in 1977, the Pat Metheny Group. His music is both loved and hated in the jazz community; some think his work is too close to light rock, but few can deny the tonal beauty and suave phrasing of his playing.

Metheny grew up in Lee's Summit, a small town outside Kansas City, Missouri. He started playing trumpet but later switched to the guitar. By the time he was fifteen, he was playing gigs with some of the best jazz musicians in Kansas City. At eighteen, he became the youngest teacher ever at the University of Miami. In 1974, when he was nineteen, he joined vibraphonist Gary Burton's group. Under his mentorship, Metheny progressed rapidly as both a leader and a musician. It was also at this time that he became one of the youngest teachers ever at Boston's Berklee College of Music. In 1975, Metheny released his first album, *Bright Size Life*.

There is no setting that defines Metheny more than his role as the leader of the Pat Metheny Group. Their first album, *The Pat Metheny Group*, was recorded for the ECM label in January 1978 in Oslo, Norway. Metheny was twenty-five at the time. Dan Gottlieb appeared on drums, Mark Egan on bass, and Lyle Mays on keyboards, including a synthesizer. The quartet's playing is precise, their solos are brief and articulate, and the songwriting is lyrical and melodic. Many hundreds of nights on the road gave the band ample opportunity to perfect their sound before going into the studio to record.

Two of the CD's most enduring songs are collaborations with Mays. The floating "San Lorenzo" has a subtle Brazilian groove, and the progressive "Phase Dance" is a fusion anthem. "Jaco," a light funk number, is Metheny's tribute to his friend and favourite bass player, Jaco Pastorius.

But make no mistake, this is Metheny's album. His playing is reverberant, lyrical, and melodic. At the time, he was reinventing the traditional guitar sound for a new generation of players, developing a way of playing that was modern in conception and its use of new technology and bold ideas but grounded deeply in the jazz tradition of melody.

■ _____

ECM #1114

■

RICHIE COLE, b. 1948
Hollywood Madness
Recorded in Studio City, California, April 25, 1979

Even as a child, Richie Cole was no stranger to the music business. He learned a great deal about it by staying up late and watching the musicians who played in his father's jazz club in Trenton, New Jersey. He learned to play the alto sax, and as a teenager, Cole's talent won him a scholarship from *Down Beat* magazine to attend the prestigious Berklee College of Music in Boston.

Cole quit Berklee after two years and paid his road dues playing in the big bands of Buddy Rich, Lionel Hampton, and Doc Severinsen. From 1975 to 1979, Cole worked with vocalese pioneer Eddie Jefferson as his musical director. Through the long days and extensive travel of touring, the two became close, and Jefferson soon became a mentor for Cole. As they drove from gig to gig in Cole's van, they began developing an idea for an album of songs that had some connection to Hollywood.

Hollywood Madness was recorded in just one day in April 1979. The repertoire is vibrant and humorous, and Cole's alto sax has an authentic bebop sensibility throughout. But what makes the album is the wise choice of guest singers. Tom Waits puts in an appearance, four songs feature the Manhattan Transfer, and Eddie Jefferson is heard on three.

Most of the songs have some connection to Hollywood. There is no better way to start than with Johnny Mercer's classic "Hooray for Hollywood." Cole's rendition is buoyant and clever. On "Relaxin' at Camarillo," written by Charlie Parker, Eddie Jefferson is delightful as he improvises lyrics about Parker. Cole's

Latin-flavoured version of Randy Weston's "Hi-Fly" is an unexpected turn. The appearance of Jefferson and the Manhattan Transfer in the final chorus is a vocalese treat. Cole's original "Tokyo Rose Sings the Hollywood Blues" is a beautiful ballad and raises the question why it has not become a standard. *Hollywood Madness*'s finest moment occurs with "Waitin' for Waits." Here, Eddie Jefferson's vocal chops are fearsome, and he has plenty of old-school charm. He makes this song his personal property. In one of the best musical punch lines, Tom Waits does put in an appearance at the end to answer why he has been late. However, it is Cole who brings it all together with his breezy, unhurried playing, balanced lyricism, and relentless swing.

Why Cole hasn't been able to repeat the inventiveness and charm found on this CD in the last twenty-five years is baffling. The concept, songs, and choice of musical guests were all airtight. But the record's magic lies in the sum of all the music parts. Cole was never able to recapture it, for as it turned out, it was Eddie Jefferson's last session. Two weeks later he was gunned down in front of a Detroit nightclub.

■ ————————————————————————

Muse #5207

S T E V E S W A L L O W , b. 1940
Home
Recorded in New York City, September 1979

Steve Swallow is one of the cleverest innovators in jazz today. He is a restless and versatile musician with a knack for doing the unexpected and for moving in any direction, from free-form to bebop. He has an appealing penchant for making his electric bass sound like a guitar by playing it in the upper register.

Swallow originally started on piano and trumpet, but while he was attending a New England private school, he started playing acoustic bass and discovered jazz. He often played with his classmate Ian Underwood, who achieved success as a member of Frank Zappa's group, the Mothers of Invention. Swallow went on to study composition at Yale, and for a brief time he entertained thoughts of becoming a poet. He changed from acoustic bass to electric in 1970. His fondness for words remains and he cleverly named Pat Metheny's CD *As Falls Wichita So Falls Wichita Falls* and one of his own live albums recorded in London, *Always Pack Your Uniform on Top*. From 1972 to 1974 he taught at the Berklee College of Music in Boston.

Over the years, Swallow has played or recorded with Dizzy Gillespie, Pat Metheny, Art Farmer, Paul Bley, Gary Burton, Joe Lovano, John Scofield, Jimmy Giuffre, and Stan Getz. His music has been sampled by A Tribe Called Quest, and he's also co-produced several albums for his wife, the pianist and bandleader Carla Bley.

He's a musician's musician and has been known from time to time, when he sees an appealing bass backstage at a jazz festival, to play a few notes on the low E string just to feel the instrument vibrate against his stomach.

Swallow joined the Stan Getz Band in 1965 but left less than two years later to play with his friend Gary Burton in Burton's quartet. Their musical partnership has continued to this day. Swallow has contributed several songs to the jazz standards repertoire, most notably "Falling Grace," "Hotel Hello," and "Eiderdown." Composing can be a long process for him, and he sometimes sits at the piano for as long as ten hours waiting for inspiration to strike, but an idea always comes.

The seeds for *Home* grew from a 1976 grant Swallow received from the National Endowment for the Arts to set the words of poet Robert Creeley to music. Creeley had been one of Swallow's favourite poets since the 1950s, and at one point Creeley's daughter babysat Swallow's children.

. *Home* is a near-perfect album with an all-star cast that includes singer Sheila Jordan, sax player Dave Liebman, drummer Bob Moses, and pianists Steve Kuhn and Lyle Mays. Liebman's tenor sax work is one of the most developed and distinct sounds on the album. Kuhn's piano playing is imaginative and virtuosic. Liebman and Kuhn's solos are poetically powerful and help to define the overall sound of *Home*.

The ten poems include "Ice Cream," "Echo," "In the Fall," "Some Echoes," and "Home." As lyrics, the poems are appealingly sparse, and Sheila Jordan sings them glacially slow so their full beauty can be relished.

Swallow's goal was to write music that suited each poem, and he was able to do just that. His compositions are exquisite and add flesh and colour to Creeley's enduring poems.

■

ECM #1160

■

MILT JACKSON, 1923–99
Ain't But a Few of Us Left
Recorded in New York City, November 1981

Ain't But a Few of Us Left is one of the best albums Milt "Bags" Jackson ever recorded. It is billed as a Jackson CD, but it is less about him than an encounter of four masters: Jackson on vibes, Oscar Peterson on piano, Ray Brown on bass, and Grady Tate on drums. It is a marvellous testimonial to the delight of making music and, as the title implies, a tribute to the golden days of jazz, the days of Ben Webster, Billie Holiday, Lester Young, Charlie Parker, and Coleman Hawkins.

It was Peterson who first drew my attention to this CD. In January 2003, he arrived for an interview with it in hand. He said, "I keep this CD in my car to listen to. I marvel at the conversation, the feeling and the intensity we had. There's a feeling when something is going well. Everything meshed perfectly. It just flowed on the title song."

Peterson's comment takes on meaning when you consider the musicians who appear. Milt Jackson was one of the founders of the Modern Jazz Quartet and is considered one of the four top vibraphonists. Grady Tate played drums on recordings by Stan Getz, Wes Montgomery, Jimmy Smith, Nat Adderley, Tony Bennett, Ella Fitzgerald, Benny Goodman, and Count Basie and was a strong and steady timekeeper. Ray Brown was a major presence in jazz from the 1950s until his death in 2002. He was highly versatile and at home in a number of settings. Oscar Peterson is one of the greatest pianists in jazz.

Ain't But a Few of Us Left features six selections recorded in one day in New York City in 1981. When Brown and Tate were late for the start of the session, producer Norman Granz, who wanted to make use of the studio time, recorded a duet with Jackson and Peterson. "A Time for Love" is Johnny Mandel's beautiful ballad and on it both Peterson and Jackson's playing is cool and sweet.

The quartet is present for the remaining songs, "Stuffy," "Body and Soul," "If I Should Lose You," and "What Am I Here For?" The title song, "Ain't But a Few of Us Left," is worth the price of the CD. It is seven minutes and twenty-six seconds of glorious jazz played by four confident musicians, who enjoy one another's company and love the music. Brown and Tate lay down a perfect rhythmic bottom end so the soloists can do their thing. Jackson is a good listener who plays with a fluid clarity, and Brown and Peterson speak a common language that comes from decades of playing together.

■

Concord/Original Jazz Classics #785

◧

DAVE FRISHBERG, b. 1933
Classics
Recorded in Stroudsburg, Pennsylvania, April 1981 and
December 1982

Dave Frishberg is a brilliant tunesmith, a songwriter's songwriter,
and some of the best singers in jazz, including Shirley Horn, Anita
O'Day, Tony Bennett, and Rosemary Clooney, have recorded his
songs. His topics include social conventions, baseball stars, and
high-rollers. Frishberg's lyrics feature a witty wordplay that is
often satirical and tongue-in-cheek.

His best-known composition, "Peel Me a Grape," was based
on Mae West's famous decadent request from the 1933 movie
I'm No Angel. It was made popular by Blossom Dearie and later
Diana Krall.

Born in St. Paul, Minnesota, Frishberg began piano lessons at
age eight but went on to study journalism at university. After a stint
in the air force he moved to New York in 1957 and started playing
freelance gigs with bands led by Ben Webster, Carmen McRae,
Mel Torme, Jimmy Rushing, Gene Krupa, and the Al Cohn and
Zoot Sims Quartet. He is no slouch at the piano, and there are
some who would be happy had he stayed a pianist and not gone on
to compose and sing his own songs.

Classics consists of seventeen songs drawn from two albums
Frishberg recorded for a small independent label in 1981 and 1982.
He's backed by two members of Phil Wood's group: Bill Goodwin,
who produced and played drums, and Steve Gilmore on bass.

There is a story behind each of the songs. As a student,
Frishberg once watched Stan Kenton's band packing up after a

college date in Minneapolis. He overheard one of the musicians say he needed to get some "Zs." Frishberg thought it was the hippest thing he'd ever heard and later wrote the song "Z's."

"My Attorney Bernie" was written as a gift for a lawyer friend in Minneapolis who played drums with Frishberg in university. His real name was Tim, not Bernie.

"Van Lingle Mungo" is baseball nostalgia and was named after the famous Dodgers pitcher of the 1930s and 1940s. It consists of nothing but the names of baseball players. "I'm Hip" is a clever parody on what it takes to be a cool guy. Frishberg had the lyrics but no melody; Bob Dorough came up with the musical setting.

Not a trained singer, Frishberg's vocal style produces an eccentric half-singing, half-speaking, nasal sound, and his piano playing swings and has a loose stride feel. But the CD is an essential because this is a genius songwriter at work.

■──

Concord #CCD-4462

□

OLIVER JONES, b. 1934, WITH SKIP BEY,
1937–2004
Then and Now
Recorded in Montreal, 1985 and 2001

Pianist Oliver Jones is one of Canada's finest jazz musicians. He's received three honorary doctorates, the Order of Canada, the Martin Luther King Award for excellence in music, the Oscar Peterson Award from the Festival International de Jazz de Montréal, and both Felix and Juno awards. But few knew of him until 1980, after he moved back to Montreal to work as a full-time jazz musician, starting in a duo with bassist Charlie Biddle. He had spent the previous sixteen years in relative obscurity in Puerto Rico, working as the musical director and pianist for Jamaican singer Kenny Hamilton. Since his return to Canada, he has been a fixture at the Montreal Jazz Festival, which Biddle helped found, and he attributes his success in large part to the exposure the festival gave him.

Jones has a distinct blues-based piano style, but there is no mistaking Oscar Peterson's influence on his playing. The similarity is quite intentional and a great compliment to his mentor. Jones grew up in the St-Henri district of Montreal, a few blocks from the Peterson home, and as a child, Jones would sit on the Petersons' porch listening to the teenaged Oscar receiving piano instruction from his sister Daisy. It was an important initiation for Jones and he later studied piano with Daisy for twelve years.

Jones was fifty years old when his first jazz album was released in 1984 on Justin Time, a small independent Montreal label. In a business that is notorious for lack of loyalty, Oliver has remained with Justin Time for twenty years and has recorded fifteen albums with them.

The sessions with bassist Skip Bey for *Then and Now* took place fifteen years apart. The first five songs were recorded in 1986, when Jones was extremely busy touring and recording. The last five were recorded in 2001, when he had slowed down and was in semi-retirement.

This is a relaxed album played by two old friends who sound confident and unconcerned about current music fads. One can imagine them sitting casually in the studio talking about which songs by their favourite artists they should include.

Erroll Garner's *Concert by the Sea* comes to mind when you hear their version of his song "I'll Remember April." Perhaps Basie or Julie London inspired the unhurried and whimsical rendition of Neil Hefti's "Girl Talk." There's a heartfelt tribute to one of the shrines of jazz, "Lullaby of Birdland," and beautiful renditions of "Somewhere Over the Rainbow" and "Old Folks."

Jones and Bey make beautiful music together. They play fast and loose and each has the chops to give the other what's required. It is a mark of their virtuosity and the staying power of the music they selected that the sessions sound as if they were separated by a day, not fifteen years.

Throughout *Then and Now*, Skip Bey is a good, steady sideman and great collaborator. Sadly, this is one of the few sessions Bey recorded. He died in 2004.

Justin Time #180

■

VARIOUS ARTISTS: HERBIE HANCOCK, DEXTER GORDON, CHET BAKER, ET AL.
'Round Midnight
Recorded in Paris, 1986

There are few jazz movies and even fewer good ones. *'Round Midnight* is one of the good ones. It is the story of an American saxophone player (Dale Turner) living in Paris in the 1950s who becomes friends with a Frenchman (Francis Borier) who worships Turner and tries to stop him from using drugs and alcohol. The jazzman character, played by Dexter Gordon (who was nominated for an Academy Award for his performance), is an amalgam of jazz musicians Lester Young and Bud Powell. The movie is based on a book titled *Dance of the Infidels* by Francis Paudras, who in the late 1950s became friends with the tragic Powell when he lived in Paris and on whom the Francis Borier character is based.

The film was innovatively directed by Bernard Tavernier, who showed empathy for his characters. A large part of his brilliance was defiantly casting jazz musician Dexter Gordon in the starring role. Another smart move was hiring Herbie Hancock to produce the soundtrack for the movie. The music is an integral part of the overall look and feel of *'Round Midnight*, as Hancock and other musicians are featured on screen. The soundtrack won the 1987 Academy Award for Best Music, Original Score.

Most of the music for the film was recorded live on the set. Hancock assembled a stellar group of musicians, including himself on piano, singer Bobby McFerrin, vibraphonist Bobby Hutcherson, vocalist and trumpeter Chet Baker, trumpeter Freddie Hubbard, drummer Tony Williams, saxophonists Dexter Gordon and Wayne

Shorter, bassist Ron Carter, pianist Cedar Walton, and guitarist John McLaughlin.

The songs suit the 1950s feel of the movie because they are well-known jazz standards. Monk's "Rhythm-A-Ning" and "'Round Midnight," Jimmy Rowles's "The Peacocks," Gershwin's "How Long Has This Been Going On?," plus "Body and Soul" and "Fair Weather."

The moody rendition of the title song, "'Round Midnight," features the unique McFerrin on vocals, sounding like a muted trumpet. "Body and Soul" is a mournful ballad with the movie's star, Dexter Gordon, on tenor sax. "The Peacocks," with Wayne Shorter playing soprano saxophone, is wistful and engaging. The playful duet "Minuit Aux Champs-Élysées" is with Hutcherson on vibes and Hancock on piano. Actress Lonette McKee's rendition of "How Long Has This Been Going On?," a poignant version of the standard, features Gordon and Hancock as accompanists.

The soundtrack's highlight is the slow rendition of Kenny Dorham's "Fair Weather." Hancock's piano playing is reflective, and Chet Baker's lingering vocals and trumpet are rightly fragile.

Removed from the context of the movie and left to stand on its own merits, the soundtrack Herbie Hancock and the musicians he collaborated with makes for a deeply moving and enduring album.

Sony BMG #CK 85811

◻

CHET BAKER, 1929–88
The Last Great Concert: My Favourite Songs, Vols. 1 & 11
Recorded in Hanover, Germany, April 28, 1988

Chesney Henry "Chet" Baker Jr. had movie-star good looks, a breathy, spine-tingling singing voice, and produced a warm melancholy sound on the trumpet. He was an enormously gifted musician who, for almost his entire adult life, put getting high on heroin above everything else. Chet never had a bank account; he always kept all of his money, no matter how much it was, in a money belt he never took off.

He was born into a musical family in Oklahoma and raised in California, and his first break came when he played with Charlie Parker during his tour of the West Coast in 1951. Baker subsequently joined the Gerry Mulligan Quintet, and his solo with them on "My Funny Valentine" became his signature. By 1954, Baker had won the *Down Beat* Jazz Poll, beating out Miles Davis, and he soon formed his own group, which became central to the creation of the West Coast cool jazz sound. Then Baker's addiction got the better of him, and years of trouble followed.

Baker died in the early morning hours of May 13, 1988, in Amsterdam. He either fell or more likely jumped from a second-storey window at the Prinz Hendrik Hotel after bingeing on pure cocaine. He was fifty-eight years old.

Amazon.com lists 251 CDs under Chet Baker's name, and therein lies a problem. Many of the recordings are of dodgy quality, because Baker recorded quickly and frequently when he needed money to get high. In his later years, he signed away the rights to many of his albums for small cash advances. Since his death, his estate has been diligent in initiating legal action against record companies they feel took advantage of him.

The Last Great Concert: My Favourite Songs, Vols. 1 & 11 is not one of those quickie albums. Recorded on April 28, 1988, in Hanover, Germany, it features Baker accompanied by sixty-one musicians from the NDR Big Band and the Hanover Radio Orchestra.

This is a beautifully balanced CD of fourteen selections spread over two discs. The old sad standards, such as "I Get Along Without You Very Well" and "I Fall in Love Too Easily," come to life; he makes them his own again. His version of "My Funny Valentine" is breathtaking. The notes flow softly and gently from his trumpet. His voice is frail. Although no one knew it at the time, the concert was his own farewell tribute. Two weeks later he was found dead on the sidewalk in Amsterdam.

■———————————————————————

Justin Time #8425/6-2

HARRY CONNICK JR., b. 1967
When Harry Met Sally
Recorded in New York City, June 1989

Pianist and singer Harry Connick Jr. has been underrated by some jazz critics and musicians, in part because he has not stayed true to jazz, playing funk in the mid-1990s and acting in a number of Hollywood movies, and in part simply because of his fame and fortune. But he is a good instrumentalist who loves playing jazz piano. An arrangement with Columbia Records allows him to release instrumental jazz albums for Marsalis Music, a label founded by Connick's childhood friend, saxophonist Branford Marsalis. Much of the music he's recorded for the label is esoteric, but it is nonetheless very satisfying, reminiscent of Thelonious Monk and Erroll Garner.

Connick came by his love of jazz naturally. He was born in the birthplace of jazz, New Orleans. His father was the district attorney for New Orleans for twenty-seven years and his mother was a Louisiana Supreme Court judge. Both his parents loved music and owned a record store. His father also played piano and recorded independent albums. Connick Jr. started playing piano at age three and later was heavily influenced by several New Orleans pianists, in particular James Booker. As an impressionable child, he sat in with these musicians in the French Quarter while his father waited outside till the wee hours to take him home. Connick eventually studied with the noted jazz patriarch, pianist and educator Ellis Marsalis. When was nineteen, he signed with Columbia.

As Connick's profile grew, Bobby Colomby (co-founder of Blood, Sweat and Tears and a record company executive) suggested to movie director Rob Reiner that Connick do the soundtrack for his 1989 comedy *When Harry Met Sally*. The movie was a hit, the soundtrack sold over two million copies around the world, made Connick a star, and earned him his first Grammy for Best Jazz Male Vocal Performance.

The soundtrack album consists of several vocal standards, including "It Had to Be You," "Don't Get Around Much Anymore," "But Not for Me," and "I Could Write a Book." Connick sings them with style and, much the way Sinatra sang, with an icy detachment. The most rewarding songs are the four instrumental tracks, "Autumn in New York," "Stompin' at the Savoy," "Winter Wonderland," and "It Had to Be You."

The big band arrangements by Marc Shaiman are lovely and grand. Connick's rhythm section, with Ben Wolfe on bass and Jeff "Tain" Watts on drums, and a guest appearance by saxophonist Frank Wess are impressive. Musically, they are a very comfortable place for Connick and show him to be an articulate singer.

When Harry Met Sally is the high point of Harry Connick Jr.'s career.

■ ───

Sony BMG #CK 45319

■

JOE HENDERSON, 1931–2001
Lush Life: The Music of Billy Strayhorn
Recorded in Englewood Cliffs, New Jersey, September 1991

Joe Henderson was lured into jazz by one of his brothers (he had fourteen siblings) who had a few *Jazz at the Philharmonic* 78s. As their cool sounds unfolded, Henderson discovered the world of great saxophonists, such as Lester Young, Illinois Jacquet, Coleman Hawkins, and Wardell Gray. Henderson was precocious musically and by the time he was nine he was playing the Lester Young saxophone solos he had heard on the records.

Henderson's recording career started in 1963 when he made *Page One*, the first of five albums for Blue Note. It was a stunning debut album that produced two classic songs, "Recorda Me" and "Blue Bossa," and remains one of the best albums recorded for the label. He also worked for Blue Note as a sideman, contributing to many classic songs such as Kenny Dorham's "Uma Mas," Lee Morgan's "The Sidewinder," and "Song for My Father," by Horace Silver. His playing on the tenor sax became part of the defining sound for the label in the 1960s.

For much of his career, Henderson was overshadowed by Sonny Rollins and John Coltrane, nor was he overly ambitious: two good reasons why his records didn't sell. In the 1970s and 1980s, Henderson languished on the sidelines, recording and performing only occasionally. It looked as if, without a well-conceived album, he would fade into total obscurity.

Then, in 1991, Henderson signed with the label Verve, a giant in the jazz world. Their idea for how to position Henderson at the forefront of the jazz scene was inspired: a concept album celebrating the music of Duke Ellington's composing and arranging partner, Billy Strayhorn. Henderson and his producer, Richard Seidel, selected ten Strayhorn songs, which they recorded at the studio of legendary engineer Rudy Van Gelder. *Lush Life: The Music of Billy Strayhorn* gave Verve the right vehicle to market Henderson, and they spent heavily to promote it. The strategy worked, and Henderson became jazz's newest star.

Lush Life marks the first time Henderson recorded an album of music by a single composer, and you can ask for no stronger a musical base to select from than compositions by Strayhorn. Henderson avoided any similarity in sound to Strayhorn and Ellington's own recordings by playing the songs in a number of settings, ranging from a quintet with Wynton Marsalis, a duo with pianist Stephen Scott, to solo.

Henderson is an incredibly expressive bop-sounding improviser who puts forward numerous musical surprises in this CD. "Take the A Train" is a dancing duet, featuring the brush work of drummer Gregory Hutchinson.

"Isfahan" is also a duet, featuring Christian McBride on bass, that was written by Strayhorn in 1963 after a trip to Persia. On it, Henderson's horn sounds almost flute-like at the start before he drifts over McBride's walk on the bass. "Bloodcount," Strayhorn's last composition, is played by the quartet, featuring Stephen Scott on piano, McBride on bass, and Hutchinson on drums.

"Johnny Come Lately," "U.M.M.G.," and "A Flower Is a Lovesome Thing" are the three songs that feature the quintet, but they are primarily about the interaction of Wynton Marsalis on trumpet and Henderson on sax. There is ample give and take between the two, reminiscent of Henderson's work with trumpeter Kenny Dorham almost thirty years earlier.

Fittingly, Henderson brings it home with the last song by playing an entrancing solo version of "Lush Life."

One reason this album was so successful creatively is that Henderson received a much needed kick in the ass, if you will. The average age of the sidemen was just twenty-two, but they had no problem holding their own with a musician of Henderson's scope and experience because they had all received their start with the masters. Marsalis had been recruited by the tough taskmaster Art Blakey; Stephen Scott and Gregory Hutchinson played with Betty Carter, whose band was a finishing school for musicians; and Christian McBride (who was nineteen when these sessions took place) had already attracted fierce interest when he moved to New York in 1989, including Freddie Hubbard's. The enduring comfort of playing Strayhorn's music provides the ideal bridge over any generation gap.

■ ———————————————————————————————

Verve #3145117792

SHIRLEY HORN, 1934–2005
Here's to Life
Recorded in Hollywood and New York, August and September 1991

The *New York Times* music critic John Pareless has written, "Songs are lucky when Shirley Horn chooses them." When Horn sang, it forever changed the way you heard that song. Her intimate, whispery style could coax nectar from a ballad by digging into its depths. She is one of the greatest singer-pianists since Nat King Cole and a huge influence on Diana Krall and Norah Jones.

Her 1960 debut album, *Ember and Ashes*, earned her fans in high places, even though it was recorded with the small Stereo-Craft label. One fan was Miles Davis, who persuaded her to leave her home in Washington to open for him at the Village Vanguard in New York City. Davis heard in Horn's singing style an approach to music similar to his. Both are known for their discriminating use of space – the silence between the sounds. This less-is-more approach helps to create a dramatic tension, particularly in the performance of ballads.

In the audience at the Village Vanguard was producer Quincy Jones, who quickly signed Horn to Mercury Records. But Horn was uncomfortable as the standup singer Mercury wanted her to be, and she left the label, retreating to her hometown of Washington, D.C., to raise her daughter and play in local clubs. She did not make another record for thirteen years, but then in 1978 she made her first album as pianist-singer with Steeplechase, a small European jazz label.

Through hard work, Horn's career took off in 1982 after she played brilliantly at the 1981 North Sea Jazz Festival in the

Netherlands, and she had a second stab at fame when she signed with Verve in 1986. She recorded numerous acclaimed albums and received nine Grammy nominations. She won in 1991 for "I Remember Miles," her tribute to Davis. The albums for Verve placed her firmly in the pantheon of the finest singer-pianists in jazz.

Here's to Life was number one on the *Billboard* jazz chart for seventeen weeks after it was released in 1992. It is dedicated to Miles Davis, who agreed to perform on two selections. Sadly, Davis died before the sessions took place.

Horn sings eleven time-tested standards and rediscovered classics. Rodgers and Hart and the Gershwin brothers are represented with "You're Nearer" and "Isn't It a Pity." There are three sweeping ballads by Johnny Mandel: "Where Do You Start?," "A Time for Love," and "Quietly There." The last two feature Miles Davis's replacement, Wynton Marsalis, on trumpet. Horn is expressive beyond words and lives in every corner of the songs.

Artie Butler's composition "Here's to Life" is one of the all-time great melodies. It is an elegant, melancholy song that toasts dreamers and their dreams. Horn's rendition is a career-defining performance, arguably the finest of her career. It is the sound of a woman who has lived the words and sings them from the centre of the song. Producer Mandel's lush orchestration creates a warm bath for her voice.

Horn could swing but she liked to go slow. Her gift was her ability to deliver a ballad's lyric in a glacially slow manner. The *Washington Post* writer Richard Harrington once described Horn's as a "whispery voice that conjured cashmere and cognac."

The last few years were rough on Horn as her left foot had to be amputated because of diabetes, but still she continued to play at major jazz festivals. She dealt with arthritis, breast cancer, and a stroke before dying of diabetes on October 20, 2005.

■ ───

Verve #000238436

BILL FRISELL, b. 1951
Have a Little Faith
Recorded in New York City, March 1992

Guitarist Bill Frisell has quietly been practising his craft for decades. He's a contemporary jazz musician who plays a blend of jazz, folk, rock gospel, country, classical, and even brass-band marches. His enviable repertoire of styles has made him much in demand, and he has worked with artists as varied as Elvis Costello, Ginger Baker, Ron Sexsmith, and the Los Angeles Philharmonic Orchestra, among many others.

Frisell played clarinet as a child in Denver, Colorado, but he became interested in guitar in high school after he listened to a lot of surf music and English rock on the radio. Then he saw the great jazz guitarist Wes Montgomery play live, which had a huge impression on him. He attended the Berklee College of Music in Boston (Pat Metheny was a classmate) and later took lessons from guitar virtuoso Jim Hall, whose influence can be heard in Frisell's technique. In 1978, he moved to Belgium where he toured with trombonist and composer Michael Gibbs and recorded as a sideman for the European label ECM Records with German bassist Eberhard Weber and Norwegian saxophonist Jan Garbarek. He returned to the States, to New York, the following year, but made his first album in 1982 for ECM.

To date his best jazz recording is his 1992 release, *Have a Little Faith*. It is a tribute album presenting his interpretation of the music of a number of American composers who have inspired him. The CD's most ambitious work is Aaron Copland's seven-movement "Billy the Kid," which Copland wrote on commission in 1938 as a score to a ballet about the American outlaw. Frisell's interpretation runs the emotional gamut from emptiness and loneliness to turmoil. The melody is sublime and Frisell emphasizes the score's rhythm and texture. The Americana theme continues with dramatic and slightly comical performances of "The Saint-Gaudens in Boston Common" by Charles Ives, John Phillip Souza's "Washing Post March," and Stephen Foster's "Little Jenny Dow."

The selection of material is as varied as the sounds Frisell creates on his guitar, and his acknowledgement of modern pop music is bold and substantial. Madonna's "Live to Tell," Nat King Cole's "When I Fall in Love," John Hiatt's "Have a Little Faith," and Bob Dylan's "Just Like a Woman" provide some of the CD's most intriguing moments. Frisell is a brilliant voice on the guitar. Sustained notes with digital delay and reverb have become his trademark sound.

Have a Little Faith is a highly successful creative endeavour. The wide range of material could have complicated the album and made it sound unappealing, but Frisell keeps it together with his arrangements, his multi-layered sound on the guitar, and the high level of musicianship of his band, in particular Don Byron on clarinet and Guy Klusevsek on accordion.

■ ──

Nonesuch Records #79301

JAN GARBAREK, b. 1947
Twelve Moons
Recorded in Oslo, Norway, September 1992

A story Jan Garbarek has told many times but still enjoys telling is how in 1961, at the age of fourteen, he heard John Coltrane's music on the radio at home in Oslo, Norway, and then taught himself to play the tenor saxophone. He was hooked on Coltrane, but soon he was exploring and appreciating the sax music of Pharaoh Sanders, Albert Ayler, and Archie Shepp.

In 1962, Garbarek won his first music competition. Scandinavia's relative lack of racial prejudice at the time made the region home to several black American jazz musicians, so there were opportunities for Garbarek to hear other saxophonists play, including Ben Webster, Dexter Gordon, and Johnny Griffin. When he was eighteen, a gig with composer and pianist George Russell kickstarted Garbarek's musical career. Russell was obviously impressed by his playing, because he asked the young man to join his band.

In 1968, Garbarek's profile soared when he was selected to be the Norwegian participant in the European Broadcasting Union festival, as broadcasts of the festival brought him wider recognition across Europe. By 1969, he had caught the attention of producer and perfectionist Manfred Eicher, who was putting together his new label, ECM. He asked Garbarek to be one of the first to record an album.

Garbarek's haunting, icy sound, punctuated with silences and long tones, helped to define ECM. His relationship with the label has been long and fruitful, and has seen Garbarek recording more than fifty CDs, both as a leader and a sideman. Some of his collaborators have included trumpeter Kenny Wheeler, guitarists Ralph Towner and Bill Frisell, bassman Charlie Haden, sitar player Ravi Shankar, and the multi-instrumentalist Egberto Gismonti. It was the recordings he made as a member of Keith Jarrett's group in the 1970s that helped make him famous.

Twelve Moons was ECM's five-hundredth release. On other recordings that feature his ambient, sometimes meandering New Age compositions, Garbarek's playing can be annoying, even grating, particularly when he plays in a higher register, but on Twelve Moons he keeps it dreamy and richly melodic. He is kept afloat by the support of an impressive group of musicians: Rainer Bruninghaus on keyboards, ECM veteran Eberhard Weber on bass, Manu Katche, who gained prominence playing for Peter Gabriel and Sting, on drums, and Marilyn Mazur on percussion. There are also vocals by Agnes Buen Garnas and Mairi Boíne.

Most of the usual Garbarek ingredients are present. He plays both soprano and tenor saxophones and blends jazz with stark Nordic imagery. The album features a combination of reflective, moody music with elements of jazz, ambient, and other selections that can trace their origins to Norwegian folk music. They are most noticeable on "Darvanan," "Huhai," and "Psalm." "Witchi Tai To" (a song he first recorded in 1974) is stunningly beautiful, with moments when his sax sounds like a muezzin's call to prayer.

Twelve Moons is a truly original record, the dazzling high point of Garbarek's long career.

ECM #1500

ROB MCCONNELL, b. 1935
Our 25th Year
Recorded in Toronto, March 1993

Rob McConnell is one of the larger-than-life figures in Canadian jazz. He's crusty, comical, and a musical triple treat, for he is an exceedingly gifted valve trombonist, arranger, and composer.

For most of his professional life he has lived in Toronto, with the exception of a brief time in Los Angeles in the late 1980s. He's been a member of Maynard Ferguson's band and Phil Nimmons's 'N' Nine Plus Six, where he was mentored by the clarinetist himself. As a leader, he's formed various sizes of big bands, from a tentet all the way down to the trios and duos he's fronted with bassist Neil Swainson, guitarist Ed Bickert, and multi-instrumentalist Don Thompson. He's been nominated for a Grammy seventeen times, winning three, had multiple Juno nominations and wins, and in 1997, he was inducted into the Juno Jazz Hall of Fame. McConnell's most defining musical moments are the work he did with the largest big band he fronted, the Boss Brass, a group he formed in 1968 and disbanded in the late nineties.

Although the Boss Brass was only ever a part-time effort, over the years it was in existence, the band was his main vehicle for jazz expression and for most of his impact on the international music scene. He turns standards into his personal property, and his compositions are fun and filled with unexpected changes. His writing makes tough demands of the musicians.

Our 25th Year was recorded in 1993 and features a twenty-two-piece big band that includes many of Canada's most accomplished musicians, among them founding Boss Brass members Ed Bickert,

Don Thompson, flautist and saxophonist Moe Koffman, flugelhorn player Guido Basso, and drummer Terry Clarke. Together,
they nurture McConnell's lyrical flights.

All of the songs are displays of effortless melody and polished
group interplay. "T.O.2" is a swinging song dedicated to Ted
O'Reilly, former host of the *Jazz Scene* on CJRT-FM and close
friend of McConnell's. McConnell's swinging "Broadway" was
inspired by an arrangement Bob Brookmeyer wrote for Gerry
Mulligan in the 1960s. The song "4 B.C." is a tribute to Benny
Carter for his eightieth birthday and features both McConnell and
saxophonist Rick Wilkins. Wilkins also contributed the arrangement for Bill Evans's "Imagination," a standard by Johnny Burke
and Jimmy Van Heusen, featuring Guido Basso on flugelhorn.
Basso's solos are central to the sound of the Boss Brass.
"Imagination" delivers *Our 25th Year*'s exceptional moment of
grace. There are lots of dark chords and a melody-rich solo by
pianist Don Thompson.

■————————————————————————————

Concord #4559

BILLY STRAYHORN, 1915–67
DUTCH JAZZ ORCHESTRA
Portrait of a Silk Thread: Newly Discovered Works of Billy Strayhorn
Recorded in Hilversum, the Netherlands, January 1995

Billy Strayhorn was an innovative composer and arranger who started to write his most popular song, "Lush Life," when he was only seventeen. Born in Dayton, Ohio, Strayhorn grew up in Pittsburgh and studied classical piano at the Pittsburgh Music Institute before turning to jazz, a genre that, unlike classical music in the 1930s, allowed black pianists to flourish. Over his lifetime, he contributed many other songs that have become standards of the jazz repertoire, including "Chelsea Bridge," "Take the A Train," "Passion Flower," "Day Dream," and "A Flower Is a Lovesome Thing." He was so gifted and productive, it is highly likely we would have heard of Billy Strayhorn even if he hadn't been associated with Duke Ellington. But, except for one brief period in 1955, Strayhorn worked for and with Ellington from 1939 until his death from cancer and alcohol in 1967. It was one of the most creative and celebrated alliances in all of jazz, and their collaboration was so close, it is not easy to differentiate their sounds. Their association left Strayhorn largely out of the limelight, which he may have preferred as an openly gay man in an era when homosexuals were expected to stay closeted.

Strayhorn was the antithesis of his employer: shy, humble, and unassuming. What they shared was prodigious talent and a very prolific nature. According to some reports, Strayhorn wrote at least one piece a week during the thirty years that he worked with

Ellington. It was more than the Ellington Orchestra could hope to play, because Ellington also composed frequently. Very difficult choices had to be made, and many of Strayhorn's songs never appeared in the Ellington songbook. The unrecorded, handwritten scores, hundreds of them, are some of Strayhorn's finest work. It is only recently that Strayhorn has begun to be recognized as a giant of jazz, a recognition he never sought nor was granted in his lifetime.

Portrait of a Silk Thread: Newly Discovered Works of Billy Strayhorn, by the Dutch Jazz Orchestra, is the first recording to document the richness of this material. The orchestra decided to record Strayhorn's compositions after being approached by musicologist Walter van de Leur, who studied the fifteen hundred scores in the Duke Ellington Collection at the Smithsonian Institution to identify Strayhorn's compositions. The CD features the orchestra performing twelve Strayhorn compositions, written between 1940 and 1967, including eight that finally received their premiere recording twenty-eight years after Strayhorn's death.

Strayhorn excelled at composing and arranging romantic ballads. "Wounded Love" was intended for a now long-forgotten theatre show; it is a gorgeous ballad with a lyrical melody. The title song, "Portrait of a Silk Thread," is a metaphor for Strayhorn himself. Like a silk thread, Strayhorn was almost invisible in Ellington's shadow, but he was strong and capable of weaving beautiful and intricate patterns. "Blue Star" is one of the CD's most glorious moments and makes one wonder why it was left out of the band's book. The DJO, led by Jerry Van Rooijen, performs the material precisely as Strayhorn would have wanted.

Strayhorn worked within a very small, closed circle of his equals, and wrote with the individual musical personalities of the soloists in the Ellington Orchestra in mind, so it is no surprise then that the DJO, a sixteen-piece big band, sounds like Duke Ellington's Orchestra. They are to be applauded for their efforts.

At a time when ghost and repertory bands are popular, the DJO has raised the musical bar. Their treatments are respectful and bring out the beauty and nuances of Strayhorn's compositions.

■

Challenge #70089

■

MARK ISHAM, b. 1951
Blue Sun
Recorded in Los Angeles, released 1995

If you don't recognize Mark Isham's name, there is still a good chance that you've heard him and not known it. Isham has composed the music for more than seventy films, including *Crash*, *Men of Honour*, *Never Cry Wolf*, *A River Runs Through It*, *The Majestic*, and *Miracle*.

He has incorporated a wide range of musical styles in his scores – in addition to the traditional orchestral approach – using big band swing, ambient music, avant-garde jazz, and world beat. To date he's received a Grammy and an Emmy and has been nominated for both Academy and Golden Globe awards.

Isham is a musical renaissance man. He says his musical awakening happened one day in 1966 when he was listening to a San Francisco jazz station and Cannonball Adderley's "74 Miles Away" came on.

As a trumpet player, Isham's experience is wide and varied. He has led jazz bands, played in the Oakland and San Francisco symphonies, and moonlighted in others' jazz bands. As a session musician, he's recorded or toured with Charles Lloyd, the Beach Boys, Pharaoh Sanders, Bruce Springsteen, Willie Nelson, Joni Mitchell, Van Morrison, and the Rolling Stones.

Isham has recorded numerous soundtracks and full-fledged jazz recordings. Several of them are remarkable albums, especially *Vapor Drawings* from 1983, his first solo album, the moody *Blue Sun*, recorded in 1995, and *Miles Remembered: The Silent Way Project* from 1999, his tribute to Miles Davis. Of the three, *Blue Sun*, the first acoustic jazz album he recorded, is the best. It is a flawless CD that has a huge emotional impact. It was selected by *Down Beat* as one of the top albums of the 1990s.

Isham's compositions are moody and cool, with many perfectly shaped musical phrases that hang in the air. It is obvious he has been influenced profoundly by Miles Davis's musical vision, for it is Davis's belief that less is more that has informed Isham's use of space, silence, and texture.

Isham is an excellent communicator, and here he is given strong musical accompaniment by his band: David Goldblatt on piano, Steve Tavaglione on tenor sax, Doug Lunn on electric bass, and Kurt Wortman on drums. Isham primarily plays the trumpet (but also the cornet and flugelhorn), on which he improves and expands the vocabulary of the instrument.

There's one standard, "In a Sentimental Mood," and eight originals. The tribute to Miles Davis, "And Miles to Go Before He Sleeps," is one of the standout tracks. It is masterpiece of mood and texture. The title track, "Blue Sun," features exemplary ensemble playing. Overall the music is whispery, romantic, and haunting. It is a good combination of contemporary jazz and old-fashioned cool.

■ ───────────────────────────

Columbia #67227

CASSANDRA WILSON, b. 1955
New Moon Daughter
Recorded in Woodstock, New York, released 1995

Cassandra Wilson has received countless media accolades, including *Time* magazine's 2001 pick for America's Best Singer. Her smoky, almost carnal delivery is delightful. She's an artist who likes the unusual and has built her reputation as a singer who likes to push musical boundaries, much like her musical influences: Joni Mitchell, Nina Simone, and Betty Carter.

Since 1993, Wilson has been an important part of the Blue Note label and has helped introduce jazz to a wider audience. Prior to signing with them, she was a well-regarded singer, but her critically acclaimed albums for small labels had left her slightly on the sidelines of the traditional jazz world. Blue Note gave her the budget, resources, and artistic licence to move forward and to make stronger statements.

It is difficult to choose between her 1993 Blue Note debut, *Blue Light Till Dawn*, and her sophomore release with the label, *New Moon Daughter*. Both are satisfying, but my preference lies with *New Moon Daughter*, primarily because of the repertoire.

In 1995, Wilson travelled to Woodstock in upstate New York to record *Blue Light Till Dawn*. The studio was in a barn that had been converted years earlier by Bob Dylan's manager, Albert Grossman. With her Harlem neighbour Craig Street on board as producer, they recorded seven covers and five originals. Wilson's blues-based compositions provide a glimpse into her southern heritage. "Little Warm Death" is a raw, powerful blues, accented perfectly with violin, about sex. "Until" is a song Wilson wrote in the hope it would be used in the Arnold Schwarzenegger movie *Junior*. "Solomon Sang," another original, is based on a story from the Bible about Solomon and Makeda, the Queen of Sheba.

Hoagy Carmichael's "Skylark" is the highlight of the album, and Wilson sings it beautifully. She captures the essence of the song with a passionate statement about longing and melancholy. Her version of Hank Williams's country classic "I'm So Lonesome I Could Cry" is heartbreaking. "Strange Fruit" is a song identified with just one singer, Billie Holiday. Wilson's rendition is bold and brave and massages the powerful imagery in the song. She is not without a sense of humour; completely out of left field is her playful version of "Last Train to Clarksville," a song first performed by the Monkees. Wilson's sensual reading of "Harvest Moon" makes it the love song that Neil Young had trouble communicating in his original.

Wilson is a great talent who moves in the jazz world with command and conviction. It is difficult to pigeonhole her musically. Her brilliance lies in blending songs from the worlds of rock, folk, pop, Tin Pan Alley, blues, and jazz, in taking songs by U2, Neil Young, and Son House and mixing them with the standards of Billie Holiday and Hoagy Carmichael.

Miles Davis once said that for jazz to stay relevant it has to reflect the time it comes from. Cassandra Wilson knows it.

Blue Note #32861

■

JOHN SCOFIELD, b. 1951
Quiet
Recorded in New York and Los Angeles, April 1996

John Scofield has repeatedly won honours as the top electric guitarist in *Down Beat*'s critics' and readers' polls. He's a versatile player who has worn a number of musical hats over the years. Perhaps this need for change comes from his time playing with Miles Davis, where he learned the importance of being a musical chameleon and being perpetually challenged musically.

Scofield's work ranges from the plugged-in jamming of *Up All Night*, to the full orchestral setting of *Scorched*, a collaboration with British composer Mark-Anthony. There is a duets CD with Pat Metheny called *I Can See Your House from Here* and a funky rhythm and blues homage to Ray Charles, *That's What I Say*. He has also recorded razor-sharp jazz-rock jams with Medeski, Martin and Wood on *A Go Go*, and the high-wire interaction of a small, closely knit band in the heat of a concert on *EnRoute*.

After leaving Blue Note, Scofield's first release for Verve was the 1996 orchestral CD *Quiet*, which is all too frequently ignored among the musical highlights of his long career. Scofield accomplished two major firsts for himself on *Quiet*: he played a nylon-string acoustic guitar and was accompanied by a horn ensemble for which he wrote the arrangements. On most records, the horns are overdubbed after the album is recorded, but Scofield and the ensemble recorded at the same time. He wrote the music for the horns and guitar as equals.

Many of Scofield's faithful fans were surprised when they listened to *Quiet* because playing an acoustic guitar gave him a new sound. He was turned on to the instrument while working with Pat Metheny. Scofield was skeptical at first when Metheny suggested he try playing acoustic, but then the softer, more intimate sound grew on him.

As well as the horns, Scofield is accompanied by a chamber orchestra, including French horn, flute, bass clarinet, and tuba. The repertoire shows Scofield delving into complex voicings and impressionistic arrangements – some are reminiscent of a Gil Evans arrangement.

From the opening of "After the Fact" to the final notes of "Away," *Quiet* is an elegant success. There is a quiet intensity to the music that makes it a meditative and tranquil pleasure. Scofield's old friends and longtime musical partners, bassist Steve Swallow and drummer Bill Stewart, help out, and Wayne Shorter plays tenor sax on three selections written specially for him. Shorter's contributions are a joy.

I can think of no more appropriate title for this release than *Quiet*. Scofield is a musician of remarkable depth and virtuosity. His guitar work is fluid and lyrical, with no raucous riffs. The calibre of the musicianship is flawless.

■ ───────────────────────────────────

Verve #3145331852

■

CHARLIE HADEN, b. 1937
Beyond the Missouri Sky (Short Stories)
Recorded in New York City, April 1996

Throughout his long career, Charlie Haden has striven for musical excellence and variety. He is one of the world's best improvisers, and his bass playing has set a standard for several generations of jazz artists.

It is no surprise that Charlie Haden became a musician. His family's country band, the Haden Family Singers, had a radio show and they were regulars at Nashville's Grand Old Opry. Charlie joined the family business at the age of two, when it was discovered he could harmonize with the songs his mother sang around the house. When he was fifteen, a bout with polio paralyzed part of Haden's face and his vocal chords, making it impossible for him to control his pitch when he sang. Then a Jazz at the Philharmonic tour came to town, and Haden saw Charlie Parker play for the first time. He became hooked on jazz and started playing the bass. In the mid-1950s, he moved to Los Angeles and soon found work as a bassist.

Musical style has never been an issue for Haden. He has played in a wide range of mainstream and experimental jazz settings, including sessions with John Coltrane, Carla Bley, Paul Bley, Keith Jarrett, Jan Garbarek, Ginger Baker, and Ornette Coleman. He's also recorded with Ringo Starr, the blues harmonica player James Cotton, and classical composer Gavin Bryars.

The projects with his bands, the Liberation Music Orchestra in the 1970s and Quartet West in the late 1980s, and collaborations with Hank Jones, Kenny Barron, and Gonzalo Rubalcaba have taken many stylistic directions, none of them standard to jazz. His music is experimental, what is known as "free jazz," and incorporates styles from Africa and Latin America. It has also been quite political.

Haden suffers from tinnitus (a ringing in the ears and a sensitivity to sound). Those who have seen him perform live recently have no doubt seen him standing behind a Plexiglas shield to protect his ears. Since being diagnosed, he plays in quieter, more subdued settings, such as a duo.

One of Haden's most rewarding duo albums, *Beyond the Missouri Sky (Short Stories)*, was recorded in 1996 with his friend guitarist Pat Metheny. It is a highly lyrical CD that gently reveals the expansive emotional heart of thirteen ballads. Although eighteen years separates Haden and Metheny in age, they share many of the same experiences. Both grew up in small towns in Missouri, Haden in Forsyth and Metheny about a hundred miles north in Lee's Summit. Both practised for hours, staring out at the vast Midwestern landscape. Both have a love of country and pop music.

The CD's soul is bared in four songs: "The Precious Jewel" was made famous by the Delorme Brothers, a group whose use of harmony influenced many in country music; "The Moon Is a Harsh Mistress" is by Jimmy Webb; "He's Gone Away," an old song that Haden's mother used to sing on the family radio show in the 1940s under the title "The Railway Man"; and the main theme for *Cinema Paradiso* by Ennio Morricone. In time, others' songs, including Johnny Mandel's "The Moon Song," Henry Mancini's great "Two for the Road," and "Spiritual," a composition by Haden's son Joshua, were added.

Haden and Metheny create gorgeous lyrical sounds on *Beyond the Missouri Sky*. Their playing has depth and profundity, and they make it sound effortless.

■ ───────────────────────────────

Verve #3145371302

MARC JOHNSON, b. 1953
Sound of Summer Running
Recorded in New York City, 1997

There are several astonishing bass players in jazz, but the bass is seldom the instrument the audience wants to hear up-front. Its role is important to the musicians in the group and is not readily clear to the uninitiated fan. In music, there are three key elements: rhythm, melody, and harmony. The bass's role is to lay the foundation for two of these: rhythm and harmony.

One of the best at doing this is Marc Johnson. Over the past twenty-five years, he has played bass on more than one hundred albums, working with some of the most creative musicians in jazz, such as Bill Frisell, Joe Lovano, Stan Getz, and Michael Brecker.

Johnson is just one of many musicians who gained their entree into jazz as a member of the Woody Herman Band. He joined the group in 1977 and played alongside saxophonist Joe Lovano and drummer Jeff Hamilton. Then a late-night visit to a club in New York City in 1978 resulted in an invitation from pianist Bill Evans to sit in with his trio at the Village Vanguard. The informal audition was successful because Johnson joined the Evans trio and remained with him until Evans's death in 1980. Johnson appeared on six Bill Evans albums, including the Grammy Award–winning *We Will Meet Again*.

Johnson's confidence grew through playing with a stylist of Evans's calibre, and he learned what was required to excel in the field. His sense of timing improved, and his knowledge of harmonics expanded. After Evans, he worked with the John Abercrombie Trio, recorded with Scofield, Lovano, and Frisell, and released several solo albums for the ECM, Verve, and JMT labels. *Sound of Summer Running* from 1997 is the most exciting recording. It features Johnson on bass, Joey Barron on drums, and guitar virtuosos Bill Frisell and Pat Metheny on acoustic and electric guitars.

The album explores some of the roots that musicians of their generation share in rock, folk, and pop, and blends them with jazz. It is a delicious collaboration. Johnson's playing is soft and rich, Metheny and Frisell have big musical personalities yet they complement one another beautifully, and Joey Barron is unobtrusive and the perfect accompanist.

Having big names, such as Pat Metheny and Bill Frisell, play on your record doesn't guarantee there will be magical moments. What it does do, because of their advanced skill, is increase the creative opportunities.

The album's standout tracks are three Johnson compositions, "Summer Running," "Ding-Dong Day," and "Porch Swing." The first is a buoyant and flowing showcase for Metheny and his forty-two-string Picasso guitar. It is so good and typically Metheny, it sounds as if it could have been a track left off one of his own records. "Ding-Dong Day" is a good-natured introduction to the many musical genres offered up on the album. It is a Ventures-meets-Chet-Atkins-meets-Wes-Montgomery potpourri, featuring jangly rock and roll and country pickin', with jazz as the adhesive that holds it all together. The laid-back "Porch Swing" is a beautiful reflective piece that features strong melodic lines from Metheny, Frisell, and Johnson.

On *Sound of Summer Running* Marc Johnson has created both a showcase for his own and others' virtuosity. He plays with warmth and poignancy, and like all great bass players, knows his place, never getting in the way. Johnson has made a great record, one that is very satisfying to listen to.

■

Verve #3145392992

DIANA KRALL, b. 1964
When I Look in Your Eyes
Recorded in New York City, 1998, released 1999

Diana Krall is possibly the most successful artist in the history of jazz. Her sultry looks, laid-back vocal delivery, prodigious piano chops, and savvy marketing have made her albums consistently top of both the jazz and pop charts. Many jazz critics have reacted negatively to the slick packaging and marketing, but it has helped her achieve a level of success that was previously attainable only by pop and rock musicians. For an artist so successful, she remains humble and unassuming, and gives the impression that she's not comfortable with the attention she's receiving and would rather be anonymous, playing piano in a combo at an after-hours club in New York City.

Krall grew up in Nanaimo, British Columbia, where she started taking piano lessons at age four and played in her high-school band. Her family figured prominently in her musical development, particularly her father, who was a huge fan of Fats Waller's music. As her talent became more obvious, word spread quickly about the piano prodigy from Nanaimo and she received a scholarship to study at the prestigious Berklee College of Music in Boston. Later her friend and mentor Ray Brown advised her to go to Los Angeles and study with Jimmy Rowles. It was good advice. Rowles had accompanied Billie Holiday, Ella Fitzgerald, and Peggy Lee and had vast knowledge about singing and playing the piano. Rowles's own laid-back, slightly melancholy vocal delivery had a huge impact on Krall.

Krall's knowledge of music is extensive. She is a musical story-teller and has a strong commitment to the lyrics of each song. She excels at recreating classic songs for today's audience. Her 1998 CD, *When I Look in Your Eyes*, is a sensual masterpiece featuring twelve late-night songs that cover the many moods of love.

The title track, Leslie Bricusse's "When I Look in Your Eyes," is a largely forgotten song from the 1967 movie *Dr. Doolittle*. Krall's orchestrated version is so much her own, you quickly forget that in the movie Rex Harrison sang it to a seal.

Two classics from 1936, Irving Berlin's "Let's Face the Music and Dance" and Cole Porter's "I've Got You Under My Skin," feature innovative bossa nova arrangements. Krall shapes these songs and gives them personality, but their true genius lies with the arranger and one of the producers of the CD, Johnny Mandel.

Mandel is a highly versatile musician. He has written several standards, including "Emily," "The Shadow of Your Smile," and the "Theme to M.A.S.H." One of his great strengths is knowing how to arrange music for singers. He's written for many of the best, including Frank Sinatra and Shirley Horn.

When Mandel and Krall first started discussing *When I Look in Your Eyes*, he told her that her voice was the sweet spot on a base-ball bat. To a former tomboy from Nanaimo, it was the right thing to say. Their collaboration is magical. Mandel participated as an arranger, producer, and conductor on seven of the twelve songs. He raised the musical bar even higher for Krall by introducing lush strings, quiet horns, and languid tempos. Krall rose to the occasion.

Krall also shines when she returns to her roots with a quartet or trio. From the 1950s, Bob Dorough's chestnut "Devil May Care" swings with newfound glory. From the Frank Sinatra song-book, there is the beautiful ballad "East of the Sun (and West of the Moon)." Diana's rendition is intimate and soothing.

It doesn't matter what setting Krall performs in on this CD because there are two constant elements throughout – her voice and the piano. As a vocalist, she is one of the best torch singers. As a pianist, she's confident and highly imaginative.

■———————————————————————————————————

Verve #065374

JOE LOVANO, b. 1952
52nd Street Themes
Recorded in New York City, November 3 and 4, 1999

Joseph Salvatore Lovano is a provocative and engaging tenor saxophonist who is constantly searching for new ways of expression.

Lovano grew up in a musical household in Cleveland. His father, Tony "Big T" Lovano, was a barber by day and a tenor player by night. He taught his son the basics and exposed him to the music of Dizzy Gillespie, Sonny Stitt, James Moody, and Lester Young.

Joe Lovano studied at the famed Berklee School of Music, where he met three musicians who would be future collaborators: John Scofield, Bill Frisell, and Kenny Werner. Lovano returned to the school in 1994 to receive the prestigious Distinguished Alumni Award and then again to teach in 2000.

As a young man, Lovano earned his stripes touring the world with Woody Herman's Thundering Herd, and later with the Mel Lewis Orchestra, playing the famed Monday night concerts at the Village Vanguard in New York City.

Few would argue that Lovano is one of the best saxophonists in the world. He has a distinct voice on his instrument and a very broad musical palette. He's an artist in the true sense of the word, and in pursuit of his creative dreams he has released almost twenty-five distinctively different CDs. Several of them are must-haves for the serious jazz collector, including three of sixteen he has recorded with the Blue Note label: *Rush Hour*, his collaboration with the arranger and horn player Gunther Schuller; *Celebrating*

Sinatra, a tribute to the singer; and *I'm All for You*, a collection of beautiful ballads.

If you are selecting only one CD by Lovano, then his Grammy Award–winning *52nd Street Themes* is the one to get. It is remarkable; a gorgeous acknowledgement of an influential place at an influential time in jazz.

In the 1940s and 1950s, 52nd Street between Fifth and Seventh avenues in New York City was the jazz headquarters of the world. Clubs such as the Three Deuces, Club Downbeat, the Onyx, the Spotlite, Jimmy Ryan's Bar, and Birdland all flourished in this era. On any given night, the history of jazz could be heard along this two-block stretch, where Charlie Parker, Miles Davis, Thelonious Monk, Erroll Garner, Jack Teagarden, Coleman Hawkins, Bessie Smith, Count Basie, Charlie Parker, Dizzy Gillespie, Billie Holiday, Art Tatum, Sarah Vaughan, the Dorsey Brothers, Artie Shaw, and many others frequently played the clubs.

On *52nd Street Themes*, Lovano and his nonet pay tribute to the composers and players of the bebop era, in particular pianist Tadd Dameron, who was one of the most important composers and arrangers of the time. There are five Dameron songs on the CD. "If You Could See Me Now" was his biggest hit, thanks to Sarah Vaughan. On this version, Lovano plays beautifully. Another Dameron composition, "On a Misty Night," was first recorded by Dameron with John Coltrane in 1956. Lovano's version is a rich arrangement with pianist John Hicks and Lovano soloing.

There is also a sampling of compositions from the time by others, including Miles Davis and Billy Strayhorn. Dizzy Gillespie and later Bud Powell first introduced Thelonious Monk's "52nd Street Theme" to audiences. Lovano's take starts with a great melody played by Steve Slagle on alto saxophone, followed by Conrad Herwig on trombone, and by Lovano and then George Garzone, both on tenor sax. Gershwin's "Embraceable You" is one of the most played songs from this era. The nonet's sound on their rendition is pure bebop, fast and furious, and Lovano, who is fronting a four-man sax section, plays exquisitely. Of particular note are the arrangements written by Willie "the Face" Smith. He is an underappreciated arranger whose writing exudes sophistication.

5 2nd Street Themes is an album played from the heart. Lovano brings an authentic bebop sensibility to bear, and gets to the core of the songs quickly and sublimely.

■——

Blue Note #96667

BOB BELDEN, b. 1956
Black Dahlia
Recorded in New York City, May 1–2, 2000

Bob Belden is one of the bright lights in jazz today. He has a wide and varied background, including playing saxophone with Woody Herman's Thundering Herd, the Mel Lewis Jazz Orchestra, and with trumpeter Donald Byrd. Off the road, he wrote commercials, sports themes for ESPN, and scores for television movies. As a record producer, he has worked with trumpeter Red Rodney, sax player Javon Jackson, and singer Cassandra Wilson. He's one of the world's foremost authorities on Miles Davis, and has won three Grammys for his production work on three retrospective box sets. With all these accomplishments, much of his work as a recording artist has been overlooked. The most fascinating is one he recorded for the Blue Note label, *Black Dahlia*.

The Black Dahlia was Elizabeth Short, an attractive young woman who dreamed of becoming a movie star, came to Hollywood in 1943, and wound up involved in the Los Angeles underworld. In January 1947, her nude body was found severed at the waist in an empty, weed-infested lot in Los Angeles. According to police reports, she was a drifter who often resorted to petty crime to get by, moving on whenever things went sour or the rent was due. Men played a prominent role in her life. To this day, her gruesome murder remains unsolved. Newspapers had a field day with the killing, giving her the name Black Dahlia because of her jet black hair and the stylish, dark-coloured dresses she used to wear. The name stuck, and came back with James Elroy's 1998 novel, *The Black Dahlia*.

This story of broken dreams was the impetus for Bob Belden to write a twelve-part orchestra tribute. In May 2000, Belden was joined in the studio by some of the finest New York City musicians to record this musical tour de force. The instrumentation ranges from solo piano to big band to a full symphony orchestra. The soloists include Tim Hagans and Lew Soloff on trumpet, pianists Marc Copland and Kevin Hays, and Joe Lovano and Belden on saxophones.

Belden's compositions and arrangements evoke the dark feeling of cinema *noir*. This could very well have been the soundtrack to the films *Chinatown* or *L.A. Confidential*. Each cut has a very distinct theme. In "Genesis," all the melodies in Black Dahlia's life are exposed. Tim Hagans's trumpet is mournful as it echoes the loneliness of her childhood. "In Flight" is a fast 4/4 piece, featuring Ira Coleman on bass and Billy Kilson on drums, that is played freely and represents her flight from reality. "City of Angels" is a long melody, featuring Hagans on trumpet, that expresses the joy of discovering something new. "Dreamworld," with Belden on tenor sax, creates the feeling of an illusion. "Elegy" is a suite that brings the entire album to a close and represents the end of Elizabeth's life and the beginning of her immortality.

This is a sweeping, ambitious work featuring world-class compositions and playing. Belden has taken a story of intrigue and shocking death and made it his own.

■ ————————————————————————————————————

Blue Note #23883

◧

CHARLIE HADEN, b. 1937
Nocturne
Recorded in Miami, August 2000

Bassist Charlie Haden is one of the most notable contributors to jazz of the last twenty-five years, whose ability to adapt, change, and be challenged is just one of his strengths as a musician. He is no stranger to Latin music, and in 1969, he and Carla Bley founded the Liberation Music Orchestra, whose sound infused an avant-garde jazz approach with both Spanish and Cuban influences. But his 2002 Grammy Award–winning album, *Nocturne*, marked the first time that Haden devoted an entire album to boleros – the romantic ballads of Latin America. Haden recorded it to help make the music of such great Latino composers as Arturo Castro, Cesar Portillo de La Luz, Marta Valdes, Martin Rojas, and Maria Teresa Lara better known in North America.

Haden's collaborator on the album is Gonzalo Rubalcaba, an impressively sensitive and thoughtful pianist who was born in Havana in 1963 and was only twenty-three when he first met Haden at the Havana Jazz Festival. Haden wanted to bring him to the United States to play, but he was prevented by the American embargo on Cuba. The friendship endured and they managed to appear on one another's albums. Several years ago they made plans to record an album of Latin music. By 1993, Rubalcaba was allowed to play in the United States, and in 1996 he emigrated from Cuba, eventually settling in Florida three years later.

When Haden and Rubalcaba produced *Nocturne*, they carefully selected musicians who have both jazz and Latin credentials, including drummer and percussionist Ignacio Berroa, violinist

Federico Britos Ruiz, and saxophonist David Sanchez, who is a hard bop player well versed in both Cuban and Puerto Rican music. Lara's "Noche de Ronda" features guitarist Pat Metheny, whose love of Brazilian music is well known. And the eclectic Joe Lovano, who has never run away from a musical challenge, brings his tenor sax to Rojas's "En la Orilla del Mundo," as well as to "Moonlight," "Transparence," and a medley that combines Cesar Portillo de La Luz's "Contigo en la Distancia" with Tania Castellanos's "En Nosotros."

Haden conceived *Nocturne* as an opportunity to show non-Latin listeners how great these songs are. Critics have complained that it is one-dimensional, of its sameness in sound, but its simplicity and humble tone is deceiving and a careful listening reveals just how daring it is harmonically. It is an album of considerable depth and beauty.

■ ───

Verve/Universal #4400136112

BILL CHARLAP, b. 1966
Stardust
Recorded in New York City, September 6–8, 2001

Bill Charlap is the best pianist to emerge in jazz since the mid-1990s. He is an astonishing player who has taken the best of what all the great jazz pianists have had to say and incorporated it into his own playing. This has made him a pianist with the chops to move the music any way he wants.

Charlap's roots lie in a boyhood home filled with song. Songwriters Charles Strouse, Yip Harburg, and Marilyn and Alan Bergman were frequent guests at the Charlap house. His father, Mark "Moose" Charlap, was a Broadway composer who contributed music to *Peter Pan*, *The Conquering Hero*, and *Whoop-Up*. His mother, Sandy Stewart, co-starred on the *Perry Como Show* on television, sang with the Benny Goodman Orchestra, and was nominated for a Grammy for her 1962 hit, "My Coloring Book." Not surprisingly, Charlap took to the piano and attended the High School of Performing Arts (of *Fame* fame) in New York City.

Charlap has played with many of the powerhouse innovators in jazz, among them Phil Woods, Benny Carter, Clark Terry, Jim Hall, and Gerry Mulligan. He has also had the challenging task of accompanying singers Tony Bennett, Carol Sloane, Helen Merrill, and Sheila Jordan. Charlap's first album as a leader was released in 1994, and since then he has matured nicely into a pianist of exceptional grace and style.

Stardust is Charlap's tribute to the prodigious talents of composer Hoagy Carmichael. Carmichael is a wise choice because he was not a composer of songs for the theatre, as were many of his songwriting contemporaries; instead, he composed for the jazz world.

There are eleven songs on *Stardust*, including "Georgia on My Mind," "Skylark," and "Two Sleepy People." Charlap turns in one memorable solo after another. Peter Washington on bass and Kenny Washington (not related) on drums provide the perfect support team, playing deliberate solos that feel comfortable and inventive.

Charlap has selected as guests singers Tony Bennett and Shirley Horn, sax and flute player Frank Wess, and guitarist Jim Hall to perform on *Stardust*; exceptional choices, all. Tony Bennett's languid delivery of "I Get Along Without You Very Well" has a perfect unhurried accompaniment by Charlap. Shirley Horn's wispy, bittersweet "Stardust" exudes sophistication, and Charlap's playing on this track is a model of melodic consistency.

But, the runaway guest star of the recording is tenor saxophonist Frank Wess. His sound is world-weary, and his musical ideas are exquisitely unobtrusive. His duo with Charlap on "Blue Orchids" is leisurely and inspiring.

■ ─────────────────────────────────────

Blue Note #35985

■

CHARLES LLOYD, b. 1938
Lift Every Voice
Recorded in Los Angeles, January and February 2002

In 1967, the Charles Lloyd Quartet, which included Keith Jarrett, was one of the most popular jazz groups in the world. Their album *Forest Flower: Live at Monterey* was one of the first jazz albums to sell one million copies, and *Down Beat* magazine declared Lloyd jazz musician of the year.

Born in Memphis, Tennessee, Lloyd was immersed in the city's rich musical culture and began playing the saxophone at age nine. He started playing professionally as a sideman with various blues bands, then in 1956, he moved to Los Angeles and began playing jazz with drummer Chico Hamilton and, later, Cannonball Adderley. He started his own quartet in 1966. Then, in 1968, at the height of his commercial success, Lloyd left music to live in Big Sur and teach transcendental meditation. The stress of constant touring, drug use, and a death in the family had all taken their toll.

In the 1980s, Lloyd gradually re-emerged from isolation and started to make records once again. None were particularly memorable until 1989, when he started recording a series of critically acclaimed CDs for ECM, the prestigious European label.

On Tuesday, September 11, 2001, Lloyd was scheduled to open at the Blue Note, the New York jazz club, but because of the attacks on the World Trade Center that day, the gig was postponed. In the days before and after the attacks, he and his wife Dorothy stayed at a friend's home in Greenwich Village, not far from ground zero and near one of the hospitals where the victims were being taken.

Lloyd's response to the cataclysmic events of that day was the impetus for *Lift Every Voice*. It consists of eighteen selections, including spirituals, folk songs, standards, love songs, hymns, and protest songs: 130 minutes of music spread over two CDs.

Lift Every Voice is an album of staggering depth. Lloyd plays to the heavens with a pristine spirituality on the tenor sax and flute. His selection of material is flawless. The old warhorse "Amazing Grace" sounds fresh and inspired, Billy Preston's "You Are So Beautiful," and Marvin Gaye's "What's Going On?" are powerfully haunting. This is an essential for your jazz library.

■

ECM #1832

■

JOHN PIZZARELLI, b. 1960
Live at Birdland
Recorded in New York City, September 2002

John Pizzarelli was born on April 6, 1960, in Paterson, New Jersey. At the age of six, he started playing the banjo and moved on to the guitar when he was ten. One day, he picked up one of his father's guitars and started playing along with records on the family stereo. Following in the path of his father, guitar legend Bucky Pizzarelli, he later started playing the more difficult seven-string guitar. The guitar players who most inspired him were his father, the legendary Les Paul, and Nat King Cole's guitarist, Oscar Moore. As a singer Cole, Chet Baker, Frank Sinatra, and Tony Bennett are the sources he drew from.

Pizzarelli's childhood memories include playing ping-pong with Zoot Sims and jam sessions at the house with Joe Pass and Les Paul. The intimacy he observed between his father and his musician friends helped make Pizzarelli decide to become a musician.

Pizzarelli recorded his first album, *I'm Hip – Please Don't Tell My Father*, in 1983. But his father already knew how hip his son was and was his biggest supporter and mentor in his development as a musician. Pizzarelli *fils* played numerous gigs with his father and often subbed for him when he couldn't make the gig. He would also work with Rosemary Clooney when she played New York City. Pizzarelli eventually started a trio, using the same instrumentation of piano, bass, and guitar as the Nat King Cole Trio.

Over the years, the trio has shared the stage with many great artists, including Clooney, Frank Sinatra, Dave Brubeck, Buddy DeFranco, George Shearing, and even the comedian Jerry Seinfeld.

To celebrate their tenth anniversary in September 2002, the John Pizzarelli Trio recorded *Live at Birdland*. The first disc of the two-disc recording is comprised of the trio's better-known songs; the second disc presents new material. Included are two James Taylor tracks, "Mean Old Man" and "Don't Let Me Be Lonely Tonight," Gershwin's "They Can't Take That Away From Me," Rodgers and Hart's "Manhattan," a pair of Rosemary Clooney staples, "Moonlight Becomes You" and "Will You Still Be Mine?," three older originals, and a classic rendition of "I Like Jersey Best."

What's most impressive about the two hours and twelve minutes of *Live at Birdland* is its entertainment value. Pizzarelli is in his most complementary setting, performing in front of an audience. He is a consummate performer: charismatic, humble, humorous, and, most importantly, a guitar player of the highest order. As you might expect, after playing together for ten years, the musical interaction among him, pianist Ray Kennedy, and his bassist brother, Martin Pizzarelli, appears to be telepathic. Playing without a drummer demands more from each member of the trio, and they deliver. Collectively, they have an impeccable sense of time and create a great groove.

Pizzarelli also has an encyclopedic knowledge of American popular song. The ease with which he moves around the repertoire is truly impressive. He has a story to tell about most everything, from hanging with Rosemary Clooney to visiting the Gershwin collection in Washington. His musical tribute to an aunt, "Headed Out to Vera's," is charming and comical.

There are no big musical challenges or walls to climb on *Live at Birdland*. It is a tenth-anniversary party that is pure musical entertainment from a performer who enjoys his work and understands how to celebrate.

■ ———————————————————————

Telarc #83577

■

GUIDO BASSO, b. 1937
Lost in the Stars
Recorded in Toronto, March 21–23, 2003

Guido Basso, one of the best and most influential jazz musicians in Canada, is equally at home on the flugelhorn, trumpet, or harmonica. He was "discovered" when he was eighteen by Vic Damone, while playing at the El Morocco club in Montreal, and he toured with Damone in 1957–58. And from 1958 until 1960, when he moved to Toronto, Basso worked with Pearl Bailey and the orchestra led by her husband, Louis Bellson.

Basso has extensive experience as an arranger, conductor, sideman, musical director for television and radio, recording artist, and playing clubs and concerts. Basso was a member of Nimmons 'N' Nine Plus Six, Ron Collier's Big Band, Rob McConnell's Tentet, and was a founding member and soloist in one of the most acclaimed Canadian big bands of all time, the Boss Brass. In 1994, he was made a member of the Order of Canada. For a man with so many achievements and strong demands on his time, he has remained humble, generous, and warm, making him one of the best-liked musicians in Toronto.

Basso's flugelhorn playing is pure melodicism, so pairing him with a sixteen-piece string orchestra is an obvious choice, and thanks to CBC Records it became a reality in 2003 when the CD *Lost in the Stars* was made. CBC commissioned jazz musician Phil Dwyer to write arrangements of standards and newer material, and he also composed a piece specifically for the session.

There are numerous highlights on *Lost in the Stars*. Guido's gorgeously rich solos are unhurried and melodic. Throughout, his playing is superlative and a model of consistency. Dwyer's arrangements are exceedingly polished.

The repertoire is perfectly suited to Basso. The title song, "Lost in the Stars," is from composer Kurt Weill's last complete Broadway musical in 1949 and is beautifully interpreted with an imaginative score by Phil Dwyer. Dwyer's original "Portrait of Guido" is based on Basso's solo on "A Portrait of Jenny" from the Boss Brass's *Jazz Album*. "I Can't Give You Anything but Love" is from the Louis Armstrong songbook, and Basso's soloing here is pure poetry. Antonio Carlos Jobim's "Waters of March" is played with poise and depth. Another highlight is Basso playing the harmonica on the Charles Aznavour song "Yesterday, When I Was Young."

Basso's backup group on *Lost in the Stars* – Dwyer on saxophone, Lorraine Desmarais on piano, Michel Donato on bass, and Paul Brochu on drums – make beautiful music together and are the perfect support team.

Basso received a Juno for best traditional jazz album in 2004 for *Lost in the Stars*.

■ _____

CBC Records #3007

■

WYNTON MARSALIS, b. 1961
The Magic Hour
Recorded in New York City, June 2003

Wynton Marsalis is arguably the most recognized jazz artist in the world. As a messenger of peace for the United Nations, he's become a jazz statesman, and as the artistic director of New York's stellar Jazz at Lincoln Center initiative, Marsalis has helped to lift jazz to new heights with his innovative programming. He has won nine Grammy Awards and in 1997 received the Pulitzer Prize for his oratorio *Blood on the Fields*.

Marsalis grew up in New Orleans and is the son of the acclaimed pianist Ellis Marsalis, one of the most respected jazz educators in the world. After moving to New York City in 1978, he played with drummer Art Blakey's combo. Blakey had an eye for talent, and his various bands were musical boot camps for many of the top players of the future. In 1981, at the age of nineteen, Marsalis released his self-titled debut album for Columbia. It helped to launch the "young lion's" movement in jazz and created a signing frenzy, as many major labels wooed youthful players to sign to their rosters. Two decades later, only a few of those players are remembered. Marsalis is the most acclaimed and, as of this writing, has sold seven million records around the world, recording thirty-three jazz and eleven classical albums. His dominance of jazz today, and his preference for pre-1965 jazz, has led to revived interest in jazz but also to the criticism that he has put avant-garde and fusion jazz into deep shade in North America.

The Magic Hour is the most exciting album of Marsalis's career and fully demonstrates what all the fuss has been about. It is fitting that the disc is his first for the Blue Note label, which has been the home of many great trumpet players, such as Kenny Dorham, Freddie Hubbard, and Donald Byrd. He's accompanied by a remarkable acoustic quartet featuring pianist Eric Lewis, bassist Carlos Henriquez, and drummer Ali Jackson. Wynton first met Lewis and Jackson when they were just twelve and Henriquez when he was fourteen, and has seen them develop into bright, innovative players.

The album casts a captivating spell. Marsalis's trumpet playing is to the point and always interesting. The music is stripped down and uncluttered, leaving the quartet lots of room for their improvisations. Also featured on the album are two special guests, singers Dianne Reeves and Bobby McFerrin. Reeves is featured on "Feeling of Jazz," a sweeping, slow-tempo blues song that culminates in a rousing scat-trumpet call and response. "Baby, I Love" is a bouncy, playful number featuring McFerrin on vocals. It has the heart and soul of a song that might have been recorded decades ago by Louis Armstrong. The playful "You and Me" is a soft-shoe song with handclaps and a great two-beat groove. It is the album's standout track. *The Magic Hour* is an exquisite CD from a wonderful, inspired musician.

Blue Note #91717

◨

JANE BUNNETT, b. 1956
Red Dragonfly
Recorded in Toronto, February 2004

Jane Bunnett is one of the most notable Canadian musicians to emerge in the last ten years. She is an exceptional soprano saxophonist and flautist who has made huge inroads around the world with her Latin-inspired music. Her forays into Cuban music with a series of critically acclaimed recordings with Cuban musicians resulted in her receiving a much-deserved Juno Award and two Grammy nominations. Along the way, Bunnett has kept her connection to the mainstream jazz world. She has recorded and performed with bassist Charlie Haden, soprano saxophonist Steve Lacy, singer Sheila Jordan, pianist Don Pullen, tenor saxophonist Dewey Redman, and pianist Paul Bley.

Perhaps her most personal statement is the 2004 release *Red Dragonfly*, a melodic take on folk songs from around the world that Bunnett and her husband and producer, Larry Cramer, have loved for years. There are compositions from Canada, the United States, Cuba, Japan, Brazil, and South Africa.

Bunnett and her band – Cramer on trumpet and flugelhorn, Kieran Overs on acoustic bass, Mark McLean on drums, and twenty-one-year-old Cuban pianist David Virelles – team up with the Penderecki String Quartet. The gorgeous, lush arrangements are contributed by Don Thompson, one of the most highly regarded jazz players in Canada, by former Cuban and piano virtuoso Hilario Duran, and by David Virelles.

Virelles's arrangement of the South African national anthem (from 1897), "Nkosi Sikelel'i Africa," is profound and moving.

Bunnett's playing is heartbreaking, and the Penderecki Quartet's mournful strings set the tone of a hymn. The traditional Appalachian folk song "Black Is the Colour" is a piece Bunnett used to sing in her school choir and she would later hear Nina Simone's recording. Bunnett's expansive rendition is reminiscent of Coltrane's blowing on "My Favourite Things."

The finest selection is the poignant rendition of "Witchi Tia To," a Navaho Peyote chant that native jazz musician Jim Pepper recorded in the 1960s. Bunnett's soprano work on this song is tasteful and controlled, and Thompson's arrangement is superb.

Throughout this CD there are marvellously deep pockets of lyricism. Bunnett and Cramer (he is often forgotten but plays a key role in the shaping of all of Bunnett's projects) abundantly demonstrate their flexibility and creativity. The beauty and grace of *Red Dragonfly* is constant. There is not one bad moment.

■

EMI #78055

ACKNOWLEDGEMENTS

This is my chance to thank not only those people who had a hand in helping write this book, but to all of those who have had a hand in my jazz education or who have helped me along the road. So, my thanks go to Wes Wilson and Kinzey Posen for all the years of doing the heavy lifting on *Afterhours*, the board and staff of JAZZ.FM91, James Adams, Tom Anniko, Donna Aprile, Sonia Arab, Bill Armstrong, the Aspers, Gary Aube, Brad Barker, Randy Barnard, Greg Barrett, Jaymz Bee, Ralph Benmergui, Tom Berry, John Bertrand, Dave Bird, Jenny Bradshaw, Beth and Derek Bright, Barbara Brown, Laurie Brown, Jane Bunnett, Glenda Calzado, Jane Chalmers, Casey Chisick, Holly Cole, Dianne Collins, Ravi Coltrane, Dick Cooper, Christian Coté, Michael Crabtree, Larry Cramer, Marc Crevier, Dan Donahue, Ken Druker, Kurt Elling, Alex Frame, Dave Frishberg, Jim Galloway, Sylvène Gilchrest, David Gilmour, Mike Giunta, Ken Gray, Charlie Haden, Robert Harris, Bill and Janet Hunt, Nigel Hunt, Susan Hunter, Ashante Infantry, Peggy Ingram, Molly Johnson, Oliver Jones, Marc Jordan, Steve Kane, Alan Kellogg, John Kendle, Neal Kimelman, Bill King, Bryan Klein, Diana Krall, Eric Ladelpha, Janet Lea, Anton Leo, Marc Levesque, Roger Levesque, Joe Lovano, Bruce Lundvall, Lee Major, Jeff Malcovish, Howard Mandshein, John Mang, Gren Marsh, Rob McConnell, Bob McKeown, Elaine McKeracher, Thom McKercher, Michael McKuen, Paul McLaughlin, Kerry and John McMahon, Pat Metheny, Jim Millican, Scott Morin, the late Brian Murphy, Mary Nelson, Phil Nimmons, Fay Olson, the late Stephen Ostick, Renah Persofsky, Oscar Peterson, Alain and Stanley Porter, Al Rae, Harold Redekopp, Wendy Reid, Doran Roberts, Ron Robinson, Ian Ross, Cass Sadek, Reiner Schwartz, Dave Sherman, Kenny Shields, Ben Sidran, Jimmy Silden, Denzal Sinclaire, Bill Smith, Chris Smith, Warren and Tula Stewart, Jeff Storry, Creed Taylor, Pat Taylor, Pam Tennant, Janet Thomson, Bernie Webber, Jim West, Terry and Joy Williams, Susan Wood, John Wyndels, Mahroni Young, and Kjartan, Branden, Griffin, and Ryan Hewitt.

Special thanks to the late Izzy Asper in appreciation of his quest for musical truth and beauty, and to Terry Porter, my father, who has been there for me, without question, over the years. Thanks, too, to my sons, Travis and Bram – I'm deeply proud of the two of you – and to the love of my life, Denise Porter. Your integrity and love continues to be my compass. To my editor, Dinah Forbes, words can't express my gratitude for your patience, thoughtfulness, and diplomacy.

My deepest thanks to all the musicians who create the music we enjoy so much and to the record companies for assisting in that creation. And my thanks to you for picking up this book. I hope it offers some useful guidance as you explore the treasures of jazz.